IRELAND

A book to accompany the public television travel series "Ireland with Michael" and while it is meant to be somewhat informative, it is mostly a bit of fun.

While I did try to be factual, contained here are many of my personal observations and opinions that are in no way factual.
See them as just that. Always follow through & google my suggestions.

Written by Michael Londra

Table of Contents

Introduction

So, you want to go to Ireland

These words start many an Irish story. Ireland is one of only a handful of spots around the world that is on the bucket list of anyone with a few bob in their pocket and a hint of romance in their heart. Ask any soul, and whether they have no connection whatsoever or their name is Sean Patrick Fin O'Toole, you will find the Emerald Isle on their list.

Lonely Planet, Condé Nast and the rest extol the virtues of a trip across the Atlantic and for good reason. While I get a kick out of being top spot in the world for a pint or to hear the world's sexiest accent, I do believe there are a hundred other details that should be added. This is what has prompted me to write.

You see, every day since I've arrived in America, I have been asked the question, "What should I do in Ireland?" Followed by "When is the best time to go?" "What should I wear?" (You see where I'm going here?) "Where should I go? Should I drive"? "Would I kill someone on a coach tour"? "Will I understand the accent"? "Should I tip"? "Will I insult anyone if I say no to a pint"? (Yes, by the way) All of this is fired at me ad nauseum, quite often sixty seconds after shaking someone's hand. Seriously, Tourism Ireland should have me on retainer. Actually, they are major sponsors of the TV show so in a way, they already have, and I love them for it.

Part of me wants to answer all of the above by framing an American turn of phrase: KISS (Keep it simple, stupid). But in truth, it isn't simple. While I suspect simplicity may be one of our finest qualities, actually getting to Ireland and making sure you enjoy yourself is loaded with complications.

In the next hour or two, you will learn the answers to all these questions and many more.

I should stress that if you want an in-depth travel guide, I think you might have made a mistake by choosing this book. Yes, we have lists of places and the usual basic information, but this book contains my take on what you should do to add to your trip. If you want Rick Steves, I think you should opt for Rick Steves. I love him, and he really was one of my main inspirations to make the tv show in the first place.

In all honesty, for a long while I didn't really understand the fascination. As an Irish man living abroad, I could never figure out the reason for the obsession. I, like most natives of any land, never really gave a second thought to where I was from. I lived in Wexford for my youth, blissfully ignorant of just how tragically beautiful the country is. I am not just talking about sweeping green fields and drama laden cliffs on the West Coast either. I am talking about the air, be it crisp or damp, the salty water, the earth, the potatoes and turnips in that earth and the people, all laden with ruddy beauty. That beauty isn't simple or sweet, it is complicated and involved but it is there for all the world to sample.

We don't make a fuss about it (or anything really). We detest fuss. The scenery is grand. The pubs are grand. The people, grand. Nobody is awesome. Nothing is outstanding. God forbid we should show enthusiasm. Oh, we are proud. We know what we have. We just want it treated the same way an Irish mother treats her first born son—adored but under no circumstances to the extent that they have "notions" about themselves.

We see ourselves as a market stall. Irish people want you to come sample them, but we get it: It's a big market! There are a lot of stalls. Why is that you ask? It's a tradeoff. Irish people are open to the world. We really do want you to stop by. We want your attention. We are, whether we care to admit it or not, interested in the great big world. Interested and incredibly nosey.

That famous Irish Céad Míle Fáilte[1] that you get when you arrive in the country is not exactly what you think. We welcome you because we get to learn about you and what you bring to the table. Do <u>not</u> mistake us for the eejits[2] you've seen us to be in *Darby O'Gill*.

If someone would have told me ten years ago that I would be immersed in tourism, I'd have thought they were trying to punk me. It all started about 8 years ago when a group of fans suggested that I lead a tour to Ireland. In truth I was dreading it. I can remember that first meeting at Dublin airport when Austin McCardle (my first and only CIE tour guide) and I welcomed a busload of Americans, Canadians, and Australians. I felt like I was walking the plank to certain death by all things Irish.

What happened instead was one of the most special weeks of my life—full of joy in watching the enthusiasm, spraoi[3] and more than anything else, the love for my homeland. It flipped a switch. I truly saw Ireland for the first time and what I saw was resplendent. I began annual tours home and have over those years become quite the expert (if anyone can be an expert about Ireland). Ireland is an ever evolving, vibrant, dynamic whirligig with three things being constant: Its beautiful landscape, its history, and its beautiful people.

---

[1] Céad Mile Failte* : 100,000 WELCOME
[2] Eejits* : IDIOTS
[3] Spraoí * : Irish joie du vivre

Ireland with Michael in Action!

Prologue

"This is one race of people for whom psychoanalysis is of no use whatsoever."

— Sigmund Freud

Regarding the quote above, I believe that every true Gael takes it with pride and a grain of salt. For myself, this is the absolute truth. I tried a therapist once and after two sessions he told me in a rather deflated manner, that I didn't really need it. And the reason for that? I believe that we are a people that may be "quirky" (for lack of a better term) but we certainly know who we are. The wonderful Irish novelist Edna O'Brien says of us *"When anyone asks me about the Irish character, I say look at the trees. Maimed, stark and misshapen, but ferociously tenacious."*

I wholeheartedly agree. We embrace and indeed take pride in our imperfection. We are comfortable with it. We own it and celebrate it. For within all the rough edges, the nooks and knots, we are bursting with complications.

Let's look at them.

The Gift of Gab
I never realized it when I lived in Ireland, but now, from the distance of miles and years, one thing comes front and center: We do like to talk. We can talk, full of substance or nonsense (and usually both). We can talk about absolutely nothing for hours. Complete and utter shite, all the while making it sound fascinating.

We will talk assuredly about politics without having the faintest clue of the issue at hand. So long as there is discourse, we are happy. However, don't be fooled into thinking we are blissfully ignorant. I find people in Ireland much more informed about world affairs than the rest of the world. We like news and we like The News.

We will talk with eloquence, quite often devoid of any grammar, whatsoever (as you can clearly see on this page). We will speak the words of poets, without knowing the name of the actual poet if, indeed, the words were written by any actual poet since we can all write our own (albeit devoid of form). We enjoy words. We enjoy syntax. We just don't quite use either with much discipline...or any discipline.

We like talking so much that we built a monument to it—a rock near Cork. They say that anyone who kisses the Blarney stone will have the gift of gab. In truth, if you are truly of Irish descent, then there should be no rush to make the journey, as you surely already possess the talent of talking rings around most other nationalities. No really.

We have had a lot of practice debating in our major seats of learning, and by that, I mean our pubs—the heart of it all, no matter where you are centered in Ireland. It is where you go to get your news, share your news, and make the news. More on those places, later.

With the gift of the gab comes the gift of storytelling. It just goes hand in hand with the accent and is definitely connected to the love of language. My father would (and at 84 still does) tell the tallest of tales, particularly in the presence of the gullible and more particularly if it fooled the listener. It really is his greatest joy in life.

His lovely neighbor Lorna has often been a victim of his tall-towered tales. He has told her that drug dealers were moving into the house next to her. He has told her the county council was going to put her house under a compulsory purchase order. He has told her our house was robbed (more than once). He has invented episodes that would make Roald Dahl proud. Every time with a sense of self-belief and accompanied drama to at once make her believe every syllable. It is remarkable. She knows that he's a rogue, loves him for it and still takes a turn at the drop of another new chapter. Even in his twilight years, he will be the one at the pub or social gathering that will keep the crowd entertained with vivid tales of the adventures of his youth. He told me that he had done the drywall on the Taj Mahal once and I went to school to share that gem with teachers and students alike. Is it any wonder I had no friends?

Music

Giraldus Cambrensis (Gerald of Wales) didn't have many compliments for the Irish in 1180 AD. He did however commend our musical skills.

"It is only in the case of musical instruments that I find any commendable diligence in the [Irish] people. They seem to me to be incomparably more skilled in these than any other people that I have seen."

We are most certainly musical. While we may not all play an instrument or sing, the gift of music "is there, alive and in our lives, whether you have any real musical talent or not." It usually starts with the granny getting you to sing a song, recite a poem, play a squeezebox (or melodeon as my father called it) or dance a jig. More often than not, it involves all of the above and at the same time.

In my case, it started with my Granny Carty on my mother's side. She would insist on a song when I arrived for a visit. While I had the talent, I didn't have the desire to sing. She'd often call me a "copper fastened dult" and force me to stand in the center of the parlor to hear me sing Slaney Valley for the hundredth time. I'm grateful for it now but back then I was mortified.

She asked all her grandkids to perform for her (and with 12 sons and daughters, there were plenty of them). It was what you had to do to get the candy she pulled from her housecoat as a reward.

My own father played the squeezebox. He told me that he was indeed a national title holder on the instrument. Even at five years old I realized that this was a stretch as I could tell that half of the notes, he played weren't the actual notes in the tune he was meant to be playing. That didn't matter to him at all nor did the inflated stories of his success, nor did my disbelief. To this day he swears he won many a contest playing the button accordion.

Mam sang around the house every single day of the year. Usually in the morning, always country music and never tuneless. She sings like a lark, with all the sweetness and purity of a ringing bell. She should have won every contest and would have but shyness got in the way.

Many friends have mediocre voices but that doesn't matter so much. They all still have a "party piece" which is essential for a gathering. Some recite poems, some tell funny stories, some dance a jig, but everyone does something. It is required. The worst of all things to bring to a party is talent without sharing it.

There is every chance you will happen on a pub during a session, which is essentially a gathering of musicians and singers, there to share the joy of the arts. Traditional music sessions are almost primal, religious, treated with the respect other countries give to royalty. Observe the session as such. Listen. If you need to talk, whisper. Appreciate it and if you really love it, offer to buy the musicians a pint. You'll find respect and it might even give you a chance to chat. Pub etiquette is probably as important as our constitution. I will touch on that in the pub section. Yes, there is a whole pub section.

Back to another much-mistaken assumption.

Lovers – Not Fighters

The "Fighting Irish" tag irritates us to no end. It is not who we are. The first use of the nickname "Fighting Irish" was for Notre Dame sports teams. It may have begun in the early 1900s, when legend says that a player's speech at the halftime of a football game against Michigan inspired a furious comeback. He reportedly yelled to his teammates, with names like Kelly, Moran and Ryan: "What's the matter with you guys? You're all Irish and you're not fighting worth a lick." The news reports that picked up the story attributed the victory to the Fighting Irishmen.

During the 1910s and 1920s, stereotypes and ethnic slurs were openly thrown at immigrants, Catholics, and the Irish. The press often referred to Notre Dame teams as the Catholics or worse, the Papists or Dirty Irish because Catholic immigrants largely populated the school, many of them Irish.

In North America, this has evolved, and it is believed that the Irish have strong convictions, that we fight our corner, and we like a fight. I have found this to be the complete opposite. It is generally our nature to not make a fuss. We hate to ruffle feathers. We will leave and lose out rather than complain, particularly if we're in a restaurant and our issue is with the server. We would leave having no conflict, rather than get the server in trouble. We don't like a to-do, particularly if someone from the lower ranks gets in trouble because there is a very good chance that we have been that server.

How Do We Look?

You don't really hear anyone saying that someone has an English face, or Belgian features. You never say, "He had a face like the map of Portugal."

Irish faces, however, are great works of art and testaments to our nationality, to our history and for sure, our weather. To oversimplify most of us fall into one of a few categories. I've been told more than once that I have the face of a priest. I fall into a type.

Among the types are:

The Map of Ireland: Big chin, thin upper lip, complex nose and hooded eyes. Rugged and reddened. Almost awkward.

The Colleen: Big-boned, russet headed but not quite red, like the Celtic queen, Maebh with freckles, skin as pale as milk, and cheekbones you could hang chandeliers from.

Black Irish: Paler again with no freckles and alabaster, almost translucent, the blackest of hair, so black that it is blue, said to come from survivors of the Spanish Armada, which has been disproven but it survives because all of us want to be somewhat exotic. I have 3% South American genes, so I am clinging to that connection to Spain but didn't get the black Irish look. If only. Think Colin Farrell.

The Sadness: Dark eyes and caverns underneath them that makes them look bruised and dark mouths. There is a slope to the face that makes you think they will cry at any moment, but it never happens. They seem cloaked in mystery, tristesse and heaviness.

Leprechaun: The wide faced, no upper lip, hazel eyed, and red faced. I won't get too specific because I've a few friends who will read this and recognize themselves.

I don't say this lightly. We may not have the physique of the Greeks, but we "do eyes" better than anyone. The blue is recognizable as fixed as the blue of our nation. Yes, believe it or not, the national color of Ireland is blue, not green. I have walked down Michigan Avenue, Rodeo Drive and Oxford Streets in London or Sydney and have found Irish eyes as quickly as I have found an Irish pub.

Luckily, I got those eyes and a blend of all the other looks. I have both the freckles and the tanned skin of the Spanish, the sad eyes that light up like fireworks, and the glint (there is always a glint). Ultimately though I will never be described as anything other than Irish. For that, I am grateful and extremely proud.

A Brief History of Ireland

St. Patrick

Historians have determined that Ireland was first settled about 10,000 years ago...late by European standards (always late to the party and last to leave). However, I have the attention span of a gnat so instead of a detailed history covering 10,000 years, I will give you a very abbreviated history fit for Reader's Digest or maybe a Broadway Musical to cover the highlights.

It is estimated that sometime around 4000 BC the first farmers arrived in Ireland. Farming marked the arrival of the new Stone Age. While a lot of people don't like to hear this, around 300 BC, Iron Age travelers known as the Celts came to Ireland from mainland Europe. These Celts had a huge influence on the country and still have to this very day. Many famous Irish myths go back to stories of great Celtic warriors.

The current first official language of the Republic of Ireland, Irish (or Gaeilge, pronounced GAYLE-GEH) stems from the Celtic language. You're about to realize on your trip around Ireland that this language is syncopated, heavy on consonants and close to being one of the most difficult languages in the world to pick up.

Following the arrival of Saint Patrick (yes, he too was a foreigner) and other Christian missionaries in the early to mid-5th century, Christianity harnessed the embedded pagan religion by using its love of nature to bring Jesus to the masses by the year 600 AD. Irish Christian scholars excelled in the study of Latin, Greek and Christian theology in monasteries throughout Ireland. You will see some of these monastic sites on your trip and if you don't, you must. Manuscript illumination, metalworking and sculpture flourished and produced such treasures as the Book of Kells, ornate jewelry like the Ardagh Chalice, and the many carved stone crosses that can still be seen across the country (along with fake and sometimes tacky reproductions in every graveyard in North America).

At the end of the 8th century and during the 9th century, the bold Vikings from what we now call Scandinavia began to invade and gradually settle in and mix with Irish society. The Vikings founded Dublin, Ireland's capital city in 988. Following the defeat of the Vikings by Brian Boru, the High King of Ireland, at Clontarf in 1014, Viking influence slowly faded. The Normans then arrived and made their mark in the 12th century. They built walled towns, like my homeplace Wexford, along with castles and churches. Normans also developed agricultural and commercial skills in Ireland.

After King Henry VIII (yes, the fella with 6 wives) declared himself head of the Church in England in 1534 and in 1541 he made sure that the Irish Parliament declared him also King of Ireland. From this time up to the late 17th century, an official English policy of 'plantation' led to the arrival of thousands of English and Scottish Protestant settlers. The larger plantations were in Ulster in the North. This was when the first sectarian violence reared its ugly head and became a common theme in Irish history. Ah, organized religion.

The 17th century was a bloody one in Ireland. It culminated with the arrival of horrible penal laws. These laws set about taking power away from Catholics, denying them, for example, the right to have leases or own land above a minimal value, outlawing Catholic clergy, forbidding higher education and entry to the professions, and imposing promises of conformity to the state church, the Church of Ireland. During the 18th century strict enforcement of the penal laws eased but by 1778 the Catholics held only about 5% of the land in Ireland.

In 1782, a Parliamentary faction successfully secured a better trading relationship with England and greater legal independence for the Parliament of Ireland. However, London still controlled much of what occurred in Ireland. Inspired by the French Revolution, an organization called the United Irishmen was formed in 1791 with the idea of bringing Irish people of all religions together to reform and reduce Britain's power in Ireland. Its leader was a young Dubliner named Theobald Wolfe Tone. The United Irishmen were the inspiration for the armed rebellion of 1798, much of which played out in Wexford. Despite attempts at help from the French, the rebellion failed and in 1801 the Act of Union was passed uniting Ireland politically with Britain.

In 1829 one of Ireland's greatest leaders Daniel O'Connell, (to be differentiated from Daniel O'Donnell the singing PBS star who is very much with us and just as legendary) known as "the great liberator" was central in getting the Act of Catholic Emancipation passed in the parliament in London. He secured the removal of an absolute ban on voting by Catholics and made it possible for them to become Members of the Parliament in London.

After this success O'Connell aimed to cancel the Act of Union and restoring an Irish parliament. However, this was a much bigger task and O'Connell's approach of non-violence was not supported by all. Such political issues were overshadowed by the worst disaster in Irish history—the Great Famine as it was historically called but known more appropriately now as the Great Hunger. Potatoes were the staple food of a growing population at the time. In 1845, 1846 and 1847 blight (a form of plant disease) hit potato crops nationwide and disaster followed. Potatoes were inedible and people began to starve to death. The response of the British government hugely contributed to the disaster as trade agreements were still controlled by London. While hundreds of thousands of people were dying of extreme hunger, Ireland was forced to export much of its wheat and dairy products to Britain and further overseas. Between 1845 and 1851 two million people died or were forced to emigrate from Ireland. The population of Ireland has never since reached its pre-famine level of approximately 8 million.

Daniel O'Connell

Ireland's history of emigration continued from this point onward with many Irish emigrants going to the United States of America. Most of your ancestors' stories begin life in America about this time.

There was little challenge to Britain's control of Ireland until the arrival of Charles Stewart Parnell. He became leader of the Irish Home Rule Party, which became the Irish Parliamentary Party in 1882. While he did not achieve Home Rule (or self-government), his skills in the House of Commons earned him the title of "the uncrowned King of Ireland". The impetus he gave to the idea of Home Rule changed the future.

In Ulster, the province in the north of Ireland, the majority of people were Protestants. They were concerned about the prospect of Home Rule being granted as they would be a Protestant minority in an independent Ireland with a Catholic majority. They favored the union with Britain. Unionists threatened violence for a separate Northern Ireland if independence was granted to Ireland.

A Home Rule Bill was passed in 1912 but it was not brought into law. The Home Rule Act was suspended at the outbreak of World War One in 1914. Many Irish nationalists believed that Home Rule would be granted after the war if they supported the British war effort. John Redmond the leader of the Irish Parliamentary Party encouraged people to join the British forces, and many did join. However, a minority of nationalists did not trust the British government leading to one of the most pivotal events in Irish history, the Easter Rising.

On April 24, 1916 (Easter Monday) two groups of armed rebels, the Irish Volunteers and the Irish Citizen Army seized important locations in Dublin: The Irish Volunteers were led by Padraig Pearse and the Irish Citizen Army was led by James Connolly.

Outside the GPO (General Post Office) on O'Connell Street in Dublin city center, Padraig Pearse read the Proclamation of the Republic which declared an Irish Republic independent of Britain. The Easter Rising finished on April 30th with the surrender of the rebels. Most of the public was actually opposed to the Rising, however public opinion soon turned when the British administration responded by executing many of the leaders of the Rising. All seven signatories to the proclamation were executed, including Pearse and Connolly.

General Post Office, Dublin

Two of the key figures involved in the rising who avoided execution were Éamon de Valera and Michael Collins (yes, you remember the 1996 movie starring Liam Neeson). In the December 1918 elections the Sinn Féin party led by de Valera won a majority of the Ireland-based seats of the House of Commons. On January 21, 1919 the Sinn Féin members of the House of Commons gathered in Dublin to form an Irish Republic parliament called Dáil Éireann, declaring power over the entire island.

What followed is known as the "war of independence" when the Irish Republican Army, the army of the newly declared Irish Republic, waged a guerilla war against British forces from 1919 to 1921. One of the key leaders of this war was indeed Michael Collins. In December 1921 a treaty was signed by the Irish and British authorities. While a level of independence was finally granted to Ireland, the treaty split Irish public and political opinion. One of the reasons for division was that Ireland was to be divided into Northern Ireland (6 counties) and the Irish Free State (26 counties) which was established in 1922.

The difference of opinion in Ireland caused a Civil War from 1922 to 1923 between pro and anti-treaty forces, with Collins (pro-treaty) and de Valera (anti-treaty) on opposing sides. The consequences of the Civil war can be seen to this day where the two largest political parties in Ireland have their roots on the opposing sides of the civil war—Fine Gael (pro-treaty) and Fianna Fáil (anti-treaty). A period of political stability followed the Civil War.

Under the same Government of Ireland Act of 1920 that created the Irish Free State, the Parliament of Northern Ireland was created. The Parliament consisted of a majority of Protestants and while there was relative stability for decades this was to come to an end in the late 1960s due to systematic discrimination against Catholics.

Northern Ireland is made up of six of the nine counties of the region of Ulster. Antrim, Armagh, Fermanagh, Tyrone, Down and Derry. The exclusion of the three counties, which had nationalist majorities, ensured a unionist majority in Northern Ireland but also a large nationalist minority. Ulster has always been, in some ways, culturally and socially different from the rest of Ireland. Ironically, it was in some ways the most Gaelic of Irish regions; it also was the most resistant to English rule, which is just mad when you think that Ulster is now the most loyalist, unionist region of Ireland.

The whole debacle that led to partition comes down to the failure of the Reformation in Ireland and the fact that it threw up a divide between the English, the Welsh, the Scots, and the Irish, who remained largely Catholic.

You might wonder where all the unionists came from. In 1607 with the famously known Flight of the Earls, the Gaelic lords of Ulster fled, and King James I initiated the settlement of Scottish Presbyterians in Ulster. Under the Stuart monarchy, starting with James I, land ownership in Ulster was transferred from native Ulster Catholics to mostly Scottish Presbyterians, as well as some English Protestants, through the 1600s. In the south, it was mostly English Anglican Protestants who had a lot more in common with Catholicism, and with the Catholic peasantry, than did these Calvinist Presbyterians of Ulster. That made Ulster culturally unique. There was also an intensification of Ireland's Catholic identity, especially after the famine, and a deepening of Catholicism and of Irish consciousness and Irish political identity. At the same time, even though the north of Ireland had a Protestant majority, they too had come to think of themselves as Irish. All these factors hardened Protestant suspicion in the north and their reticence to be drawn into an independent Ireland in the south.

The world war hugely complicated the situation. Most of Ireland at the outbreak of war in 1914 remained loyal to the United Kingdom. Indeed, the British Army successfully raised Irish regiments for the war on the Western Front in Europe. So, it's not true that Ireland, in general, chose this moment to rebel. It was the Easter Rebels who chose to rise up in Dublin in rebellion against British rule.

Their execution and martyrdom complicated the situation. In the south, the once-unpopular Easter rebels immediately became national heroes. But in the north, their rebellion was regarded as an act of betrayal against Great Britain in its time of desperate need, and it heightened the resolve of Protestant who had been deeply loyal to the United Kingdom during World War 1 and would not be drawn into a united and independent Ireland. The First World War led to bitter resentment against Irish republicanism in both Britain and Ulster and it made reconciliation between Ireland's Catholic and Protestant communities impossible in the aftermath of the war. It's no coincidence that the partition happened in its immediate aftermath.

The Government of Ireland Act was designed to create two separate territories, both of which would remain in the United Kingdom, made up of Northern Ireland and a Southern Ireland— each being autonomous, self-governing entities of the United Kingdom. But Irish nationalists had declared an independent Ireland and launched a guerrilla campaign, the Irish War of Independence, and refused to recognize the act. In December 1921, the British reconciled themselves to the nationalists' demands and created an Irish Free State in the 26 counties of the south. Those counties were not yet an Irish Republic; they were still part of the British Empire, but no longer a part of the United Kingdom.

Confused? That's ok. This is complicated. The Irish Free State went its own way and in 1949 became the Republic of Ireland.

Trouble began almost immediately with the way the border was drawn. The expectation at the time was that Northern Ireland would be left with the Protestant majority parts of Ulster, which only would have been four of the nine traditional counties. The thinking was that the area would simply be too small a state to be viable and that Northern Ireland would therefore eventually have to reconcile itself to inclusion within the Irish Free State. But the Irish Boundary Commission, established in the treaty ending the Anglo–Irish War, ultimately included six of the nine counties of Ulster within Northern Ireland, and that left a lot of nationalist areas like Tyrone, Fermanagh, and Omagh, all of which were Catholic-majority areas, stranded in Northern Ireland.

That fact made Northern Ireland a bigger entity than anyone had expected it to be and heightened the hatred on both sides. It resulted in a resentful Catholic minority within Northern Ireland. Northern Ireland's response to having an unreconciled, unhappy, large Catholic minority in their midst, was essentially to create a Protestant unionist one-party state, which governed with dominant force. The Ulster Unionist Party in Northern Ireland wrote into law rampant discrimination against Catholics—in housing, employment, education, and job opportunities.

Meanwhile, the Irish Republic was also effectively a one-party state, strongly committed to cultural nationalism, with a lot of influence from the Roman Catholic Church, including a heavy dose of Catholicism in the constitution. That was bound to heighten the resistance of Ulster Protestants to inclusion within anything like a united Ireland. It was a timebomb waiting to happen And, indeed, when the civil rights movement in the 1960s came along, it did, with a 30-year period of violence bringing about the beginning of Catholic civil rights marches in Northern Ireland which led to violent reactions from some Protestant loyalists and from the police force. This was a period known as 'the Troubles' when nationalist or republican and loyalist or unionist groups clashed.

In 1969 British troops were sent to Derry and Belfast to maintain order and to protect the Catholic minority. However, the army soon came to be seen as a tool of the Protestant majority by the minority Catholic community. This was reinforced by events such as Bloody Sunday in 1972, a dark day when British forces opened fire on a Catholic civil rights march in Derry killing 13 people. An escalation of paramilitary violence followed with many atrocities committed by both sides. The period of 'the Troubles' are generally agreed to have finished with the Belfast (or Good Friday) Agreement of April 10th, 1998. Between 1969 and 1998 it is estimated that well over 3,000 people were killed by paramilitary groups on opposing sides of the conflict. Since 1998 considerable stability and peace has come to Northern Ireland. In 2007 former bitterly opposing parties the Democratic Unionist Party (DUP) and Sinn Féin began to co-operate in government together in Northern Ireland.

The Good Friday Agreement, the power-sharing deal that ended the Troubles, in 1998, has diminished the distinctions between north and south. The momentum started there and a will for reunification. The strong referendum in favor of the Good Friday Agreement on both sides of the border in Northern Ireland and the Irish Republic, suggested that there was a political will, if not toward unification, at least toward reconciliation.

Will Ireland eventually reunite? The factors have changed. Protestants are no longer a clear majority in Northern Ireland. It's more evenly split, with a growing percentage of people in the north of Ireland who do not align themselves either as Protestant or Catholic, which means there is now a sizable minority who have no stake in this fight. And they don't identify with Protestant unionists nor with Catholic nationalists.

More importantly, from the 1980s onward, there was a massive liberalization in the Irish Republic, with the Catholic Church losing hold on Irish culture, education, and the state. There has been a real move toward liberalization and secularization to align the Irish Republic with the rest of Europe. It is now a place of economic progress and looks more like the rest of Europe.

In 1973 Ireland joined the European Economic Community (now the European Union or EU). Economic reforms in the 1980s along with membership in the EU created one of the world's highest economic growth rates. Ireland in the 1990s, so long considered a country of emigration, became a country of immigration. This period in Irish history was called the Celtic Tiger. We love being European and there is no chance of us leaving.

Brexit, Britain's departure from the EU has complicated our lives. Leaving means borders, economy, livelihoods are all affected. History has shown us that this causes unrest, so we are certainly at a crossroads. Personally, I am optimistic, but God knows what is ahead of us.

Music to Prepare You

There is a list of artists and specific albums that I think you should download before you fly to Ireland. They all should give you a feeling for the country.

Mary Black. Mary is my all time, favorite singer. I first bought an album of hers in 1985 and it changed my world. Nobody taps into the essence of Ireland like her. Not as a traditional singer but as a communicator. Her song choices and delivery evoke imagery of a country, ancient and modern. The music, arrangements and performances are all timeless. She is a wonder and probably the most influential artist of my life. Pick up The Best of Mary Black. Song for Ireland will tell exactly what to expect of the country.

Moving Hearts. The Storm is an album that marked a new direction for Irish music. It took traditional music and transformed it. The members of the band are idols of mine. Getting to eventually work with one or two of them was a real privilege.

The Clancy Brothers. You will probably know The Clancy Brothers. Their music has crossed borders. Respected by folk legends like Bob Dylan and Pete Seeger, they hit America in the 60s and gained a global following. Just download anything you can get of them and embrace some classic Irish songs.

The Chieftains. I can't think of a legacy I respect more. Their musicality, respect for tradition and their understanding of the importance of collaboration earned them the respect of every other genre and global super stars, not to mention a Grammy or two.

Christy Moore. The combination of humor, brilliant song choice and political commentary made Christy a legend in Ireland. He not only reflects the Irish world around him but he moves it. Irish people are political by nature but we are also funny, even when we talk about heavy subjects. Listen to Christy and learn about us.

Sinead O Connor. If your tastes lean to harder music, I would try Sinead. Her career has been complex and difficult. Yes, her commentary on the Catholic church ruined her career in the US and her choices over the years have been marked with controversy but you cannot argue with her performances. She is angry and beautiful at the same time. She interprets songs and transforms their meaning, elevates them, and makes them divine. I Do Not Want What I Haven't Got is one of the best Irish albums of all time, arguably. I love The Lion and the Cobra.

I would also add **Hozier, Clannad, The Dubliners, Enya**, and **Altan** to the mix. Regardless, who you choose, listening to our music will help you understand us more.

Map of Ireland

Planes, Trains, and Automobiles

Air Travel

Dublin serves as the largest airport in Ireland. As airports go, I love it but more on that later. Let me give you the overlay, Ireland has four main airports – Dublin, Cork, Shannon and Knock. There are also smaller regional airports at Donegal, Kerry, Galway, Sligo and Waterford. Donegal and Kerry are the ones I'd look closer at as they could come in very useful for you.

Our main airline is Aer Lingus. It is the flag carrier of the country and was formed by the Irish government. It has since been privatized. Many airlines serve Ireland with Aer Lingus, Aer Lingus Regional and Ryanair having a significant presence at Irish Airports.

North American Airlines serving Ireland include Air Canada, American Airlines, Norwegian Air Shuttle, Delta Air Lines and United Airlines. You really are spoiled for choice. You can now fly direct from the U.S. to Dublin from New York (Newark and JFK), Boston, Chicago, Detroit, Charlotte, Miami, Atlanta, San Francisco, Philadelphia, Los Angeles, White Plains and we are currently waiting for Minneapolis to return, post Covid. From all these airports you will catch a direct flight in the evening, arriving the next morning.

Ireland is well connected with Europe mainly through Dublin, Shannon and Cork Airports. The United Kingdom/Ireland route is the most travelled with flights every hour to many regional airports. You can get to anywhere in Europe quite easily and cheaply if you plan ahead. Indeed, if you are planning a trip to continental Europe at any point in the future, I would look at routing your trip through Ireland, spending a few days in Dublin and then heading on. It is often considerably cheaper than direct flights to continental Europe and you'll get two vacations in one.

Unlike many international airports with multiple buildings, Dublin airport has just two terminals. Terminal One caters to European destinations and Terminal Two, the new shiny one, makes visitors from North America feel welcome.

There is every chance you are heading to parts that are a little further. If heading to the Northwest of Ireland, I would try Donegal airport or Carrickfinn as it is known locally. Only an hour from Dublin and with reasonable prices if you plan ahead, it is worth it. Landing in this spot on a clear day is one of the most spectacular sites, globally. The airport itself has been voted most scenic in the world more than once.

For the Southwest, I would go with Kerry Airport. Landing in the heart of the Kingdom County is just spectacular. It is quite the drive from the airport to Killarney so you might want to check if your hotel offers a shuttle service.

For Shannon airport in County Clare on the West coast you can actually fly direct from New York or Boston so that might be an option for you, especially if you want the Cliffs of Moher to be your first stop. Nearby Ennis would make a great first night.

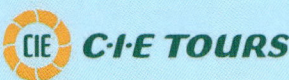

CIE TOURS

Vacations with CIE Tours:
Your Invitation to Explore

From all-inclusive guided vacations to customized private driver experiences and self-drive adventures, CIE Tours vacations appeal to a wide range of travelers – honeymooners, multi-generational families, heritage-seekers, and those simply looking to connect with people and places.

—————————— **Explore further at cietours.com** ——————————

- Sign up for email and be among the first to learn about special offers
- Read reviews from other guests
- Read our travel blog for inspiration, recipes and more
- Chat with a CIE Tours travel specialist with your specific questions

For more information contact your travel advisor or call:

Contact Center	Groups	Private Driver
800-243-8687	**800-223-6508**	**888-467-2685**

cietours.com

IRELAND | BRITAIN | ICELAND | ITALY

Aer Lingus has been bringing the world home to Ireland since 1936. If you're thinking about Ireland, Aer Lingus is ready when you are to take you home.

IRELAND IS CALLING...
Press the Green Button

Ireland is ready to welcome you. To savor the fresh local cuisine and to enjoy our soul-stirring scenery. To experience those exhilarating clifftop walks with the Atlantic winds whipping through your hair. The tiny village pub where you're treated just like family. The chance to explore those rolling green hills, dotted with mysterious standing stones and ruined castles.

It's time. Start planning, visit ireland.com

Ireland ☘

Press the Green Button

Immigration, Amenities, Baggage Claim, Currency Exchange

Regardless of where you started your trip in the US or Canada you will have flown overnight, arriving somewhere between 5 a.m. and 11 a.m. after a pretty ghastly overnighter. At that point everyone is keen to get off the flight and out into Ireland. There is a mad rush as if Armageddon is upon us, to get to immigration.

You will deplane and find yourself on the longest corridor in history to take you to immigration lines. I say take your time. The odds of long lines are slim for your flight at that hour. In general, the immigration process is simpler than getting through on the U.S. side and in truth, I find the officials to be a lot more pleasant, even at that outrageous hour.

If by chance you have a Euro passport, I would use that as I have waited no longer than 5 minutes in the many years, I have been flying in. Even with the foreign passport line, I find that it moves fairly swiftly.

If I am flying up front and have some time to spare, I will stop at the Aer Lingus lounge to start my day with a morning routine. It kind of sets me up for that first day. There are plenty of bathrooms en route to do the same. Brush your teeth, comb the hair. It will be a while until you get to your hotel.

If you need assistance because of mobility you will need to make an appointment for that at least 48 hours before arrival. If you didn't do that, I would mention it to airline staff as you board the plane. There are multiple help points around the airport if you need assistance at the last minute. Look for the blue box and press the button.

While you wait, there is every temptation to take out your phone or to start taking your first touristy snaps. This is not encouraged.

By not encouraged, I mean it is strictly forbidden and the powers that be will not be happy if you start shooting Instagram reels while in line. Keep it firmly in your pocket.

There might be a few quick questions to answer to make sure you aren't planning on staying in Ireland for longer than your allotted vacation time. It is really all fairly straight forward and pleasant enough.

You are out of immigration now and are confronted by baggage claim. Now, airports around the globe post Covid seem to have lost the realm of their senses when it comes to baggage. Long waits are the norm, globally and while I wish I could say that Dublin is better, it is not. I think over the past 2 years I have flown into Dublin about 10 times and each time the wait has been about a half hour.

While you wait you can use the currency exchange or the neighboring ATMs to withdraw from Euros in cash. However, and this is a BIG however, I would not choose the exchange. Their rates are outrageous in the airport. I now use my card pretty much everywhere I go in Ireland without a problem, but I always withdraw 400 euros to have in my pocket if something comes up. While most banks are now used to international travel and charges, each bank will differ so please know the costs involved to withdraw cash or to use your card. Some smaller banks still want to know in advance where you will be travelling so they don't block the charges. Denied, is not a word you want to hear 5000 miles away from home, even when uttered in a sexy Irish accent.

So, you have made it through immigration, and you've picked up the bags. Exit through customs using the green channel as in, you have nothing to declare. Please remember that we are European but cannabis and indeed every other drug in the U.S. is also illegal in Ireland. Get high on Guinness instead. You mightn't feel great the next day but at least you won't be in jail...well not for drug smuggling.

You are through the gate and will be faced with an ocean of expecting faces of relatives waiting on their loved one coming home after what can be sometimes years away. If you want to have your faith restored in humanity, stop a while, and witness those reunions. It is uplifting and heartbreaking all at once.

Tours and Transportation

You will now meet your tour operator driver holding a sign or you will head for a bus or rental hire. The bus people carry signs with their tour name and wear a uniform. Don't stray from this point even if you can't find them on first glance. They will be there. There is a café to the left and right, both serving a delicious full Irish breakfast, if you must wait a while.

Should you have opted to rent a car you will just be walking straight ahead to the Skybridge, You will find all the major U.S. companies along with some stranger names like Sixt, NewWay, EuropCar.

Be aware that the car pick up is off site and you will be taken by shuttle. The staff is very helpful and friendly so don't worry about that. Getting out of the area around the airport is tricky so be sure you are confident of your route and don't be afraid to ask again and again.

Car Rental

Something to note: We don't call renting a car "car rental" in Ireland. We call it Car Hire. You are hiring a car, not renting it.

Car rental usually ends up as an afterthought and the result is that many panic book without understanding the ins and outs of it. If you are going to jump in, you had better know the facts.

This is important: Renting a car in Ireland is very expensive and can be out of reach for a lot of people, especially mid-Summer. The number one issue people have when renting a car in Ireland is insurance and it would *appear* that it's been designed to confuse in order to inflate the car rental company's profit. Do you need everything they recommend?! Is it not included in the price?! Does your credit card not cover it?! So much to think about. Be sure to prepare for price comparisons and it is very important to find out all the extras they add.

The first hard fact is that you need to be over 25 to rent a car in Ireland. You also need a valid driving license (shocker!)

The next thing to think about is how will your chosen mode of transport effect your experience exploring Ireland? Do you prefer freedom or are you happy to take organized tours? Would you like the choice of going off the beaten path or are you happy to go wherever organized tours can take you?

Last and most important think about what it is like to drive on the opposite side of the car and on the opposite side of the road. Our roads in general are amazing but once you get to the villages and rural areas in order to witness something more traditional the lanes get winding and unfinished. Extremely winding and unfinished.

Some companies allow you to rent a car in Ireland without a credit card, but you need to do your research. For example, Enterprise allows you to use a Debit Card, but *only* at non-airport locations. Many Irish rental car companies won't accept debit cards and require you to have a credit card with you when you arrive at the counter.

Read everything because understanding Car Hire Excess is *very* important when renting a car in Ireland. This is a set amount which Irish car rental companies will not cover if you must make a claim.

Third-Party Cover (aka TPC, Motor Liability or Legal Liability Insurance) is included, by law, in your car rental price. This isn't an add on and the rental companies are required to add it in. However, Third Party Liability Insurance is the *minimum level of cover* that's legally allowed to drive a car in Ireland. Know what it does and doesn't cover. It will sort damage to someone else's car or property and any injury you cause to the person. It will NOT cover any medical or legal costs you have with any damage to the car you're driving

Your rental will come with Third Party Cover, but many other companies throw in additional insurance – you'll be told this before you sign the rental agreement. Again, read and ask questions.

Collision Damage Waiver is optional, and the cost is *generally* charged daily. If you buy this, make sure to see what the excess fee is. The cheaper the insurance the more you'll be left to pay.

There may be even more charges that might be sneakily added.

One load of nonsense is the Airport Collection fee only added if you pick up at the airport.

Deciding on manual v. automatic transmissions is also costly. Automatic transmissions are rare in Ireland and come at a premium.

Tolls are a thing. License plates are recorded on some of the major roads. Check www.eflow.ie

If the bus is for you let me tell you that in Ireland it is the way to go. Don't think Greyhound. Think luxury coaches with Wi-Fi. Buses can be found on the lower level of both terminals in Dublin. Signage is excellent. If you are just heading to your hotel in Dublin city, I would pay extra for the Aircoach. It has a lot more stops so it is likely you will end up close to your hotel.

Taxis

Should you want to take a taxi you are covered. While we have Uber in Ireland it will only get you a licensed taxi. I recommend stepping right out the front door of either terminal. Taxis have dedicated lanes all through the city, so they get places fast. Depending on where you are in the city it will cost between €25 and €50. The rate can rise if you are travelling on an Irish public holiday or late at night. It could also be higher if your hotel is not in Dublin city center.

Make sure your taxi driver is using the meter, mounted on the dashboard. Never agree a fixed price with a Dublin taxi driver. I mean NEVER. As soon as you get in the cab, check that he has switched on the meter.

You should know that Dublin taxi drivers are a particular breed. They can talk. Oh boy, can they talk. Dubliners make for great story tellers. Don't expect a conversation as much as a TED Talk. I will say I have never laughed so much as in the back of a Dublin taxi.

If you're travelling as a group with lots of bags to a specific location, taking a taxi from Dublin Airport to Dublin city center is a solid option as multiple bus fares will come to the same price.

Coaches

To head "down the country" as we say whether you are heading North, South, East for Wesht (the h is intentional) I recommend long haul coaches to bring you further afield. Now you can take Bus Eireann, the national bus service or use a more local company operating from the airport. In my case, I choose, Wexfordbus, a brilliant service that is comfortable, clean and efficient.

Tipping, Pub Etiquette, and The Scone

Tipping

Historically, Ireland has never really had a strong tipping culture, however, over the past ten years or so that has slowly changed. Because of globalization, travel, and the Internet, so many locals and most visitors now tend to tip for certain services, in particular restaurants, taxis and personal services (e.g., hairdressing). If you want to tip and are in doubt about how much, think 10% and you are grand. All tips are at your discretion! A rough general guide follows.

Restaurants.: A standard tip is 10%-15% of the bill, based on the quality of service. If you receive exceptional service, of course you may tip higher. WARNING. Some restaurants already add a 'service charge' on to the bill (usually 12.5%) so keep an eye out for that particularly in more tourist areas. This will be printed somewhere near the end of the bill, or you can ask your server if there is a service charge/gratuity. Most hotel restaurants include a service charge. If this service charge is added there is no need to tip as this charge is essentially 'the tip'. If, however, you get that great server it is appropriate to give them a few extra bob. I promise, you won't be offending anyone!

It is worth keeping in mind that in many cases serving staff does not receive tips which are added to cards (or in hotels those which are added to room charge). It is always best to ask in advance and tip in cash, to ensure your tip is received by staff and not the establishment. This above all upsets me about a restaurant.

Counter Service/Fast Food: No tip expected but I usually put my coin change into the cup on the counter if it is there.

Bartenders: No tip is expected and please don't just leave money on the counter. I've often found that it confuses bartenders. If you wish to tip, hand it to the barman or make sure he knows it is for him. If you are part of a large group and have had several drinks and exceptional service from the staff, you might consider a tip of a few Euros. While barmen do not expect tips, table staff do and again a few Euro for a large round is considered acceptable. It's important to remember, though, that the system for tipping in pubs in Ireland is different from that in the USA. You don't tip the barman per drink; only when buying a large-ish round, for complicated cocktails, or at the end of the night. (Or if the bartender is cute and you're trying to impress them but that's just me.)

Hotel Housekeeping/Maid Service: I usually leave a couple of Euro. Again, this may be confusing. I spend a lot of time in Irish hotels, so I try to say hello to the room cleaning staff and hand them the tip. Leaving it on the pillow is a mistake as it will be left on the pillow.

Hotel Porter: €2 per bag is reasonable.

Bed and Breakfast Staff: Many B&Bs in Ireland are family run so tipping isn't expected. In larger hotels or houses where staff are employed, I would always leave a few bob.

Taxi Driver: Tip 5% to10% of the fare if the driver has been particularly helpful, informative, and courteous. In general taxi drivers are generally surprised and delighted if you tip well. I just think it is the decent thing to do.

Organized Coach Tours: I like to tell all travelers on my tours that without the highly skilled, professional, and experienced guides/drivers, we would be wandering aimlessly around Ireland having to transport, inform, carry bags and entertain ourselves. I encourage a large tip at the end of the vacation. Hard cash. They don't want a bottle of whiskey bought at the last distillery. HARD CASH, I TELL YOU. I recommend a $100 tip or more. Yes, this may seem like a lot but these people are devoted servants for your entire vacation. Make it part of your vacation budget.

Hairdresser/manicurist: Ladies Hairdresser 10% of the bill, Gents barbers €1 to €2 Euro or 10% of the bill

Buying a Round

The pub/bar culture, like any other, has unspoken rules, no matter where they are. The Irish Pub is no different. You might have heard the term "this round is on me" and it can be confusing. Understanding the customs and terminology will ensure a good time during your visit (and keep you from being thought of as a "tight Yank"). In the pub it is essential to understand how 'buying rounds' works. Just know that in Ireland, it's standard pub behavior to buy drinks in 'rounds' if you're drinking in a group. It is best not to overthink it but this is how it plays out.

It simply means that each person will pay for the group's drinks in turn. The first 'round' of drinks is bought by person number one, then the second round by person number two. And so on and so on, until people stop drinking...and that might take a while.

It is important to recognize when a round begins. Upon entering a drinking establishment, someone will say something like "I'll get the first round, what are ye having?" This is like a contract offer. You understand the terms, the parties involved and the length of the contract.

Now, here is the tricky bit. <u>IF YOU ACCEPT A DRINK, YOU ARE IN THE ROUND.</u> I will say this again. <u>IF YOU ACCEPT A DRINK, YOU</u>

ARE IN THE ROUND. You have signed the contract. There will now be an expectation that you will buy a round of drinks, before the first person buys again. In Ireland, it is a serious faux pas to be in the round without offering to repay the round later. People are judged bigtime by this.

If the drinking ends before you get the chance to buy, you could and should offer to buy one last round, even knowing that people are leaving. They will say no but that doesn't matter. You offered. You can then and only then offer to catch them next time.

If you don't plan on drinking with this group or don't want to get into buying rounds because of budget, it's perfectly ok to decline and not get into a round in the first place. People won't bat an eye and certainly understand living on a budget in Ireland. Go with the line "I'll stay on my own, thanks".

Now there is a grey area: Irish people will often offer to buy you a drink outside a round. Being offered a drink does not mean that the person expects or will even accept one in return. I know. Grey! It is best to go with the flow.

Please know that while in the US some bartenders will buy you an occasional round, that will not happen in Ireland.

If you're with a large group, don't worry about having to buy a boatload of pints! Buying rounds in larger groups is usually only done at weddings or funerals or when an Irish tenor comes back to his hometown laden with guilt for leaving in the first place and is shamed into it by his friends. No one you know.

Ice is Not a Thing

I've come to realize that ice isn't a thing in Ireland. I don't only mean ice in a drink. I mean ice in general. When it is served, I promise you will be underwhelmed. A gin and tonic will be served with two excuses for ice cubes that are already melting into your hard-earned tipple. The cubes used are small to begin with, but they are usually half melted when they are put in the glass, so it tends to make for sad looking cocktails. Yes, things are getting better. I have found that cocktail bars understand the value of the ice cube but it's still a gamble in regular pubs.

Hotel bars are better equipped than old pubs but even then, they do not have ice machines on every second floor or indeed any floor. You will rarely find an ice bucket in your room, no matter how high end. Why would you need an ice bucket when you there's no ice? Unless you are staying at a 5 star, I would avoid calling reception asking for a bucket of ice unless you want to be ridiculed by the staff for the remainder of your stay.

If you are determined to have a few beverages in your room, I would suggest you go down to the bar and ask for a pint glass of ice. Tread lightly, prepare to be judged and bring a cash tip.

I've never quite figured the reason for this travesty. My guess is the weather. It is never that warm, so we have not learned the value of the frozen stuff.

You will have no problem getting cold drinks. The notion that beer is warm in Ireland isn't true. However, if you want to keep drinks cold in your room, you might want to invest in a foldable, soft-wall cooler to carry with you.

Scones and Soda Bread

Irish Scones

You might be wondering why there is an entire section dedicated to Scones in this book. The truth is scones are a thing in Ireland, as much as soda bread or pints. A cup of tea and a scone can solve everything. You will find, however, that for all their similarities, Irish scones and American scones are quite different. Irish scones are simpler, with fewer ingredients. American scones come in a million different flavors with all sorts of fancy icing, cinnamon, and sometimes, fancy cinnamon icing. They are much more likely to be heavily flavored. American scones are made to be eaten alone (ok...maybe with a little butter), but generally they are the flavor. They usually have a lot "going on" without any toppings added.

Irish scones have a much plainer flavor profile, and come in three kinds: plain white, plain brown and plain white with currants. They are designed to be topped with things like whipped cream, butter, and/or preserves. (I've noticed that they have started to add things like pear which sounds far too exotic for my tastes but maybe it'll beep your jeep).

You'll find that in Ireland people are particular about how they take their scones. Me, I like either a warm plain white scone with a dollop of whipped cream and Wexford strawberry jam or a raisin scone, toasted and thick with a doorstep of butter. It depends on my mood (and how much time I want to spend on the treadmill).

Either way you need to know what you are getting yourself into. It is a solid midday snack after a late Irish breakfast that will get you to dinner time.

My rule (yes, I have rules about food stuffs) is that they can only be eaten with tea. None of your latté nonsense with a scone. A 'cuppa tay' is perfectly paired with a scone. Know that it is okay to ask for plain scones if you don't like raisins. It's also okay to ask for brown scones if you prefer something with a nuttier, wholewheat flavor.

It is also important to know that is scone, pronounced "scone" (like bone), not pronounced "scon" (like lawn) which is the more British pronunciation.

Below you will find one of my favorite scone recipes. Making these will get you in the mood for your trip. It's easy and delicious. If I can make them, anyone can.

Scones Recipe

- 4 2/3 cups (1lb 8oz) Self Raising flour (keep a little extra for dusting)
- 3/4 cup (6oz) butter (keep it frozen – I'll explain below
- 3 level teaspoons baking powder
- 1/2 cup (4oz) sugar
- 1/2 cup (4oz) raisins/sultanas
- 1 1/4 cup (10floz) milk
- 2 eggs (beaten)

Add flour to a large mixing bowl.

Grate the frozen butter into the bowl. Frozen butter adds pockets of buttery goodness plus air and texture into the mix.

Stir in raisins, baking powder, & sugar.

Whisk the eggs and milk in a separate small bowl, add into the bowl, & stir until a soft dough is formed.

On a floured surface, press the scones down to about 1" thickness and then cut them out with a cookie cutter. Combine the leftover dough and repeat until you have used it all up.

Place the scones on a parchment-lined baking tray. After bringing the oven to 425 degrees, bake for 22 - 24 minutes before cooling on a wire rack.

Soda Bread Recipe

Irish Brown Soda Bread

This is my go-to soda bread recipe. It makes two loaves in a standard loaf tin, grease them well and pre heat oven to 350 degrees.

This recipe comes courtesy of Áine Lee and her mammy, Kathy. I love it toasted with a slab of Kerrygold butter on top. Again, if I can make it, anyone can.

Soda Bread Recipe

2 cups white flour
2 cups Odlums extra coarse whole meal[4]
1 cup ground flax seed
1 cup oat bran
Heaped teaspoon baking soda
Heaped teaspoon salt
¼ cup of brown sugar
Quart of buttermilk

Mix all dry ingredients well with a k blade on mixer or by hand. Add buttermilk, this should be just enough, but it should be the consistency of cake batter. Pour into the loaf tins and bake for one hour, turn off oven and leave for another 10 mins. Cool on a wire rack.

---

[4] This may be difficult to find in the U.S. It is available online through Amazon or substitute any coarse whole meal flour

The Booze of It All

Irish Whiskey was one of the earliest distilled drinks in Europe, around 1200 BC. The industry has known many ups and downs since that time. The 1990s showed a major resurgence in the industry and for the next twenty years has become the fastest growing sprit in the world.

By June 2019 there were 25 operating distilleries in Ireland with several more in the planning stages. I am listing a few of them here with the hope that it will help you develop your taste for whiskey. Our whiskey is a piece of Ireland that you can enjoy wherever in the world you may be!

The Distilleries

Jameson Distillery Bow Street
Bow St., Luas Smithfield, Dublin
(+353) 1 807-2355
www.jamesonwhiskey.com

In 1780 John Jameson opened the doors of his distillery on Bow St. Over 200 years later the doors are still open, and Jameson is known the world over. This is my go-to whiskey when I make my Irish coffees. This tour is great. Tour, taste, learn how to blend your own whiskey, master the craft of cocktail making or draw whiskey straight from a cask.

The Dublin Liberties Distillery
33 Mill Street, Dublin
(+353) 1 410-0380
www.thedld.com

The Dublin Liberties Distillery is a state-of-the-art working distillery housed in a 400-year-old mill building in the heart of

Dublin City. Visitors can see first-hand how the whiskey is made, get up close and personal with copper pot stills and hear the stories of the historic Liberties area.

Micil Distillery
www.MicilDistillery.com

Micil Distillery is the first distillery in Galway in over 100 years. It's headed up by Pádraic Ó Griallais, a 6th generation distiller passionately continuing a family tradition. The distillery traces its roots back to 1848, when Pádraic's great-great-great grandfather, Micil Mac Chearra, began producing poitín (Irish moonshine) in Connemara. Tours/tastings are a unique experience and there is a familial feeling about the place.

Kilbeggan Distillery
(+353) 0 933-2134
www.kilbegganwhiskey.com

Kilbeggan is a place full of stories worth telling. Visit Irelands Oldest Licensed Distillery to experience first- hand how the distillery has evolved since 1757 with the innovative spirit of today. In addition to sampling Kilbeggan Whiskey and Kilbeggan Single Grain, you can try Connemara, Ireland's only peated single malt whiskey.

Jameson Distillery Midleton
Distillers Walk, Midleton, Co. Cork
(+353) 21 461-3594
www.jamesonwhiskey.com

Today, every drop of Jameson is produced in Midleton and this place is impressive. This site is undergoing a massive overhaul. The tours here is the best you will find in the country. Love the place. I recently got a 21-year-old Redbreast from here that is outstanding.

Dingle Whiskey Distillery
The Old Mill, Milltown Roundabout, Dingle, Co. Kerry, V92 E7YD
(+353) 66-402-9011
www.dingledistillery.ie

The Dingle Whiskey Distillery came into being in Winter 2012. Located just outside Dingle town this distillery very much part of Dingle life. I've a soft spot for the whiskey and the people who make it. Alongside regular small batches of whiskey, they produce award-winning Dingle Vodka and Dingle Gin. The Gin was awarded the title of World's Best Gin at the World Gin Awards 2019 and I am a fan. They closed partially post Covid so check the website.

Pearse Lyons Distillery
121-122 James's Street, Dublin
(+353) 1 6916000
www.pearselyonsdistillery.com

Discover over 800 years of history and awaken your senses with whiskey tours and tastings at Dublin's only boutique distillery. Winner of the Irish Tourism Industry Award for Dublin's Best Visitor Experience 2019, Pearse Lyons Distillery, is located in Dublin's historic Liberties, Pearse Lyons Distillery, and is a five-minute walk from The Guinness Storehouse.

The Echlinville Distillery
Echlinville House, 62 Gransha Road, Newtownards
(+44) 0 28 4273 8597
www.echlinville.com

Echlinville Distillery began production in 2013, making it the first newly licensed distillery in Northern Ireland for over 125 years.

A true farm distillery, their story is one of provenance, connection to the land and devotion to the ancient art of distilling. Situated just one hour from Belfast and two hours from Dublin, Echlinville is also close to the Game of Thrones trail and just 15 minutes from the filming location for Winterfell near the shores of scenic Strangford Lough. This makes for a a whole day out...as long as you have a designated driver.

Sliabh Liag Distillers

(+353) 74 973 9875

www.sliabhliagdistillers.com

An Dúlamán Irish Maritime Gin is the first gin distilled in Co. Donegal. This premium gin is distilled by using five locally harvested varieties of seaweed, as well as six other botanicals. At the heart of the distillery sits Méabh (pronounced Mayve), a hand-hammered 500-litre copper still. Méabh, meaning "she who intoxicates" takes the botanicals and yields a gin as unique as the Donegal coast itself.

Irish Whiskey Museum

119 Grafton Street, Dublin

(+353) 0 1 525 0970

www.irishwhiskeymuseum.ie

This is one of Dublin's most central visitor attractions, located opposite the main gates of Trinity College. Journey back through time while the Irish Whiskey Museum's guides tell you the complete history of Irish whiskey. The Irish Whiskey Museum is independent of all whiskey distilleries, offering its visitors the opportunity to taste and experience a vast selection of Irish Whiskey. Whether it's Single Grain, Malt, Pot Still or a Blended Whiskey, the Museum's whiskey experts will always be able to help you find the perfect whiskey to suit your palate.

Slane Distillery
Slane, County Meath
(+353) 469-030-600,
www.slaneirishwhiskey.com

Set in the heart of the Boyne Valley, Slane Distillery is housed in beautifully restored 250-year-old stable buildings on the grounds of the Slane Castle. Visitors to Slane are guided through the entire whiskey making process from grain to glass, while learning about the traceability of the ingredients with water and barley coming from the castle grounds, coupled with their unique focus on sustainability.

The Tullamore D.E.W. Visitor Centre
Bury Quay, Tullamore, Co. Offaly,
(+353) 0 5793 25015
www.tullamoredew.com

This unique visitor experience is set in Tullamore Dew's original 19th century bonded warehouse on the banks of the Grand Canal in the town of Tullamore, Co. Offaly.

The Powerscourt Distillery
Powerscourt Estate, Enniskerry, Co. Wicklow A98 A9T7,
(+353) 1-506-5656
www.powerscourtdistillery.com

Drawing pure water from an underground lake that lies beneath the Estate, Powerscourt sets the perfect stage for distilling Irish whiskey. Housed in the mills to the side of this remarkable building and estate, the distillery is a great experience after a day of walking the estate and lunching in the great house itself. Their food historian, Santina Kennedy, is a wealth of knowledge. Tell her I said hello!

The Copeland Distillery
43 Manor Street, Donaghadee, County Down
(+44) (0) 28 9162 4000
www.copelanddistillery.com

About a half hour from Belfast, the Copeland Distillery is where
the tales of old smugglers and savage ocean battles meet the
coast of Donaghadee. As you set out on the tour you will find a
combination of the history and process of spirit making, the
history of The Copeland Islands and the heritage of Donaghadee.

Ha'Penny Gin School
Pearse Lyons Distillery
121-122 James's Street, Dublin
(+353) (0) 1-691-6000
www.pearselyonsdistillery.com or contact

If Gin is your thing, Ha'penny Gin School at Pearse Lyons Distillery
is Dublin's ultimate Gin Experience. The gin school, located on the
grounds of Pearse Lyons Distillery, is housed in newly restored
early 20 Century townhouses in the heart of Dublin's historic
Liberties Museum.

The Guinness Storehouse
St James's Gate, Luas James's
(+353) (0)1 408 4800
www.guinness-storehouse.com

The Guinness Storehouse is located in the heart of the legendary
St James's Gate Brewery in Dublin. The former fermentation plant
has been re-imagined into a visitor center, dedicated to the
history of Guinness. Ireland's number one visitor attraction
unfolds its tale across seven floors, and it is so worth. Is it
touristy? Yes. Is it fun? Definitely.

Learn how to pour the perfect pint at the Guinness Academy. The six-step ritual is as legendary as the beer itself. Be sure to experience the breath-taking 360-degree panoramic view of Dublin City in the renowned Gravity Bar. I call it the mothership for a reason.

THE MUST DO LIST

Before we get into the nitty gritty, let's look at the big picture. I often hear from people just returning from Ireland that they found it overwhelming. It is always disappointing. No matter the trip you want in Ireland, there are some essentials that I think are a must to ensure a complete baptism of all things Gaelic, the Irish "must dos" if you will. I know that this list will change as the editions of this book ensue; but for today, for this print, these are my recommendations (in no particular order)

Shopping in Ireland

Nobody thinks their budget will run past food and drink but Ireland is proving that it can stand with the best when it comes to taking your hard earned dollars. The dollar is as strong as you get these days so take a deep breath and jump in. Our craft industry is stellar and there is real access to artists' work in nearly every tourism store in the country. If you want handmade knitwear, you have most certainly come to the right spot, but we have excellent local pottery, artisan foods, paintings and sculptures readily available in every town. Be sure to ask for the local craft store. Bringing home, a locally sourced piece of clay from a potter's wheel is a different ballgame to bringing back a shamrock emblazoned on a t-shirt made in China.

"Down the Country"
www.buseireann.ie

I have noticed a trend of Americans flying into Dublin for a weekend enroute to another European capital. Aer Lingus is by far the cheapest way to get to Europe and stopping off in Ireland for a few days will save you a lot of money on your airfare. While I wholeheartedly endorse this, I notice that people think they are seeing Ireland by spending a weekend in Dublin ("the big smoke" as we call it). Dublin, while unique, is a very limited portrait of Ireland, distinctly different from the rest of the island. It's like flying to Maui and thinking you know the USA. If you have a few days, I am urging you to find a route out of the city. You can get a luxury coach in any direction to rural Ireland that will get you to another world in under 2 hours (see the Planes, Trains, and Automobiles section of this book). "Down the country" doesn't mean South. Down in this case means anywhere but Dublin. Do it.

Dingle, County Kerry
www.dingle-peninsula.ie

You will need more than a few days in Éire if you are venturing as far Southwest as the Dingle Peninsula. It is quite the drive from Dublin but once you get there, it is like opening a gate to another world of sea life, coastal drives, cliffs and mountains, jigs and reels, fine art, and finer food. They know what they've got down there and they make sure you have the best time when you get there. They understand tourism, they understand standards and most importantly they understand a good time. If you miss it on your first trip to Ireland, be sure to add it to the next one.

Take the Boat

It never fails to amuse me to witness the shock that despite every map on the planet showing us as a very definite island, people don't quite understand just how maritime-focused our lives are in Ireland. So, to understand who we are as a people get out on the water with Irish folk. You will understand us more. We are comfortable on the water, be it lake fishing on Lough Corrib, cruising on the Shannon, drifting on a barge in Carlow or kayaking on the Copper Coast. Check out adventure activities on all our coasts. Every county has a tourism site and a full listing of on-water activities.

Find your Castle

www.castlesinireland.com

Each one of us a romantic fictional character down deep inside just waiting to get out. There is something about a castle that touches the knight, lord, lady-in-waiting or jester in us all. I lean to the whimsy of life, so it isn't a stretch for me to walk the turrets anywhere, imagining my kingdom and peoples. I've seen even the coldest or most timid of hearts become someone new (or old) when entering the great hall of a medieval fortress. The history is enveloping and better still, escaping. If you truly want to jump out of your world, enter an older one by visiting one of our wonderous castles. I've been to most, multiple times and they never let me down. Switch off the cell phone, charge the battlements, reach out to touch the ancient walls, climb the circles of stairs. When history envelops you, it somehow bestows you with perspective to make the current world less stressful. Find your castle. God knows you are spoiled for choice.

The Water of Life

I list the distilleries in this book for a reason. I am new to whiskey. I have had the occasional scotch (Lagavullin was and still is my tipple) but that was rare and the tv show meant I had to start learning about our own drop. We were the first to invent it after all. Irish whiskey is now the fastest growing spirit in the vast alcohol industry. The emergence of small distilleries around the country has added a whole new field of discovery around the island. Even if you hate whiskey, the story and the process to make it is fascinating and innate to our land. You can also ask if they have their own brand of gin, which they usually do. Whether it is the massive Midleton Distillery or a tiny local one, you will have a unique experience that will give you Ireland on tap.

Guinness Storehouse, Dublin

www.guinness-storehouse.com

The Guinness Storehouse in Dublin is The Mothership. It is touristy, over the top, and loud. A boozy Disney Park of an exhibit that is entertaining, exuberant, quirky and worth every penny. The pint at the end is so satisfying and gives you the Instagram brag you wanted as soon as you landed.

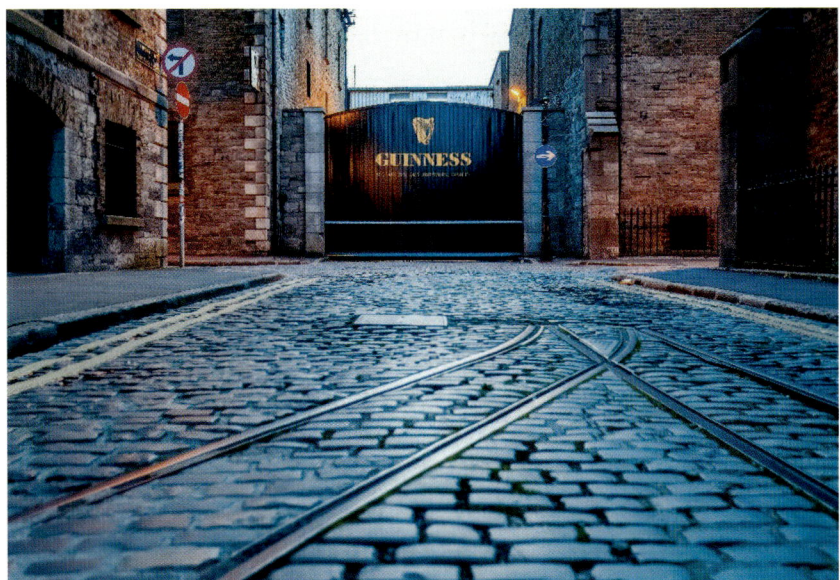

The Guinness Storehouse

The Sporting Life

www.gaa.ie

Our two national sporting obsessions, Gaelic Football and Hurling, are thrilling, fast moving experiences for players and spectators alike. I urge you to watch a game. Check out the local sports listings, no matter what town or village you are in. To me, nothing is more exciting than watching a great game of hurling. The visceral, electric atmosphere is unmatched. The speed and danger of the hard ball hurtling through the air, the clash of the ash (hurls are almost all made of this hard wood) above the players heads, the lack of any stoppages (yes, I am talking to you, American football!) and the nonstop running up and down the length of the field will leave you gasping for air. Be prepared for rainy weather, rough excuses for stadiums, bad language from the sidelines (especially if you are with me) and the time of your life. Camogie, the female version is hugely popular. Croke Park in Dublin city is the headquarters of the GAA, and as such, there is no better place to experience a big game than here. You won't get tickets to the national finals but there are games every weekend.

Hurling

The Theatre

www.irishtheatre.ie

Every small town and every city has a stage of some sort. Sometimes these small theatres can get lost when you are planning a tour. After all, you can go to your local performing arts center back in the US. Why go see a show in Ireland? Theatre life is as essential to small towns as the pubs. The arts are a part of who we are as Irish people. Not just Irish arts. Our stages present musical theater, classical Irish plays, concerts, traditional arts. The Works. For a slice of the town you are visiting, ask where the local hall is and what shows are playing. Whether it is Riverdance or Rogers and Hammerstein, I guarantee you will walk away with a better understand of Ireland. Arts Centers in many towns will have ongoing exhibitions, recitals and creative projects that channel the character of those towns, painting for you a snapshot of the artistic nature of the place.

Festivals

Irish folk love a party and each town in the country has a busy calendar of festivals all year round. So, no matter the time of the year, there will surely be a local cultural event of interest for you to attend. We can turn anything into a festival from writing to opera, from comedy to busking.

Some of the best annual festivals you should try including: The Dublin Theater Festival held every September and October, the Galway Arts festival, which takes places every July and attracts artists from all corners of the globe, the Kilkenny Cat Laughs, in June. I would also recommend the Cork Jazz Festival or the Wexford Opera Festivals.

Kenmare

www.kenmare.ie

This town is having a moment. New restaurants, hotels, galleries making the place perfect for a long weekend if you want to avoid the madness of Killarney. I was there this past month and was genuinely taken back by the energy of the place. Ideal for exploring the Ring of Kerry but without the coach-tour crowds of its more famous neighbor, Kenmare (Néidin, meaning 'little nest' in Irish) is a tidy triangle of streets making it easy to stroll around. Linger for coffee on the side of the road and watch the busy market town go by. The terrace at the newly done up Landsdowne is perfect. For hotels you've the luxurious Sheen Falls Lodge and The Park just outside the town.

Kenmare

Gardens

www.gardensofireland.ie

I am glad that finally the glorious gardens of Ireland are being feted. I think because of the wonder of the wilds on the island, the more manicured plots tend to lose out. The Irish garden is as gorgeous as any garden the English can put together. It is time they are getting their due. Most estates around the Island have permanent horticultural teams tweaking and pruning to get the most out of the temperate climate. Flowers bloom earlier and longer here. My personal favorites are Kylemore Abbey & Gardens and Wells House & Mount Congreve. Check them out.

Kylemore Gardens

Holy Houses

As a seat of learning in medieval times, the reach and footprint of Christianity on our land and its people is evidenced even now by its impact on the environment, physical, social and political. While the Catholic church has fallen from grace in recent years, it is still embedded in the fabric of the land. A trip to abbeys like

65

Clonmacnoise, Holy Cross or Glendalough will paint the historic picture for you, and beautifully. However, I would also urge you to visit the churches in every town, catholic and protestant, to understand how they have influenced the story of that town. Don't be afraid to stop a local to ask.

The Blarney Stone
www.blarneycastle.ie

Yes, it is a tourist trap and yes, at peak season you will join every other American in Ireland, but I say it is worth a morning. The stone itself is a block of carboniferous limestone built into the battlements of Blarney Castle, about five miles outside of Cork city. It was put into the tower at the castle in 1446.

For me the gardens make it a glorious day out. Take the time and the energy to walk about as much as you can to catch all the themed areas. Work up an appetite and stroll over to Blarney Woolen Mills to shop and eat in their great restaurant.

Riverdance
www.riverdance.com

Yes, I was in it and yes, I am not exactly objective. The show changed my life and changed how the world looks at Ireland. One would think 25 years later the flame would fizzle, but it has not. Every year at the Gaiety theatre just off Stephen's Green in Dublin you can see the production. It is a slightly smaller but no less as impactful a show as the Broadway version in which I was fortunate enough to sing in 2000. I promise you a great time. Nothing and I mean nothing is as vital as Bill Whelan's stellar score, and the first time you see that troupe start rolling their heads at the top of the show, you will remember my words. I will always be proud of Riverdance and the impact it has had on Irish arts and beyond, Ireland as a country.

Tombs

www.newgrange.com

Newgrange, a 5,200-year-old passage tomb located in County Meath, just north of Dublin city in Ireland's Ancient East. This can easily be done as a day trip from the city. The incredible passage was built by Stone Age farmers and has been one of Ireland's wonders for centuries. It feels like aliens descended from the heavens to build it. An incredible feature of Newgrange is a passage measuring less than an inch that leads into a chamber with three alcoves. During the mornings around the Winter Solstice annually, the passage and chamber are aligned with the rising sun, and the inside illuminates in an astonishing way. If you want to feel the ancient nature of the country, this is the place for you.

Newgrange

Wexford
www.visitwexford.ie

Yes, I am a bit keen and yes, I am not exactly impartial, but I promise if you can overlook my bias, you will have a wonderful time. Ask any Irish person where they like to go in the summer if they can't hit the tropics of Spain or Greece and they will say Wexford. The beaches are second to none, with spots like Curracloe and Rosslare hosting half of Dublin from June to September. The fresh seafood or the tasty strawberries with out-of-the cow cream are just some of the culinary delights in store for you. Add Johnstown Castle, Hook Head, the pubs, the world class opera house and the legendary nightlife of Wexford town and you have a wealth of things to do to keep you entertained for days.

Beautiful Wexford Town

Gaols

www.kilmainhamgaolmuseum.ie
www.spikeislandcork.ie

No one place in Irish has as much history of Kilmainham Gaol in Dublin. It is one of the most famous jails in the world and definitely Ireland's most notorious prison. The walls of this prison have held some of Ireland's most prominent leaders and those who evoked political change throughout Irish history. Using it as a conduit to learn our story will not let you down. The prison has also been used in many movies including the original *Italian Job* and *In the Name of the Father.* Randomly, I know for a fact the inside of the jail influenced Hal Prince when designing the Broadway set of Sweeney Todd. It gets busy in the summer. It is just across the road from the Irish Museum of Modern Art so that would make for a full day out.

Kilmainham Gaol

If you have ever been interested in San Francisco's Alcatraz, then you will love a trip to Spike Island in Cork. This island, located in Cork Harbour and has an intriguing history. In the past 1300 years, the island has transformed from a 6th-century monastery to a grand fortress, and then to a prison. Now, it is a public museum and is the perfect day trip from Cork City.

The Cemeteries
www.dctrust.ie

Glasnevin Cemetery opened in the 1839 and is a large cemetery in Dublin. It holds the graves and memorials of several notable figures, and a visit is anything but morbid. Here you can see the final resting place of Ireland's most famous leaders, including Daniel O'Connell, Charles Stewart Parnell, Michael Collins, and Éamon de Valera. Add a pint at The Gravediggers Pub nearby and you have a great afternoon.

The Cliffs of Moher, County Clare
www.cliffsofmoher.ie

Historic sites will come and go. Museums, interactive exhibitions will open and close, trendy words like ecotourism will abound, but The Cliffs of Moher will never change. It is our natural infrastructure that is the jewel in our crown. The Cliffs of Moher remains the anchor in our navy, the big gun in our army, the pyramid in our Egypt. Do not miss this place. Be it sunny, misty, windy, or snowy, the Cliffs of Moher have made the strongest of men cry. It will not disappoint.

Northern Ireland
Belfast - www.belfasttours.com
Derry - www.bogsidehistorytours.com

Taxi!!! The topic of The Troubles is nearly unavoidable if you want to understand life in Northern Ireland. While the beauty of the North will consume you, you need the history to appreciate how it got here.

The best way to start to understand Northern Ireland's complex history and how it shaped the present is by taking a black taxi tour through West Belfast or Derry. Drivers lead the tours in small groups so you are promised a unique more personal insight into the troubles and perspective on peace.

Most tours last 90 minutes and take you to some of the city's most-famous political murals, peace walls, and areas which were greatly affected by The Troubles. I guarantee you will learn so much and appreciate and be inspired by the peace accord and the people living it.

Climb Every Mountain
www.destinationwestport.com

Croagh Patrick is the arguably the most famous mountain in Ireland though it is by no means the highest, is situated near the town of Westport. Croagh Patrick comes from the Irish Cruach Phádraig meaning "(Saint) Patrick's stack."

On the last Sunday in July, thousands of pilgrims climb Croagh Patrick in honor of Ireland's patron saint who, as the story goes, fasted and prayed on the summit for 40 days. On a clear day from the top of the mountain, you can take in incredible views of Clew Bay and the surrounding south Mayo countryside. It usually takes two hours for the average person to reach the summit, and one and a half hours to descend. You need to be fit for this, but it is worth it.

If climbing to the summit is not for you, make Westport your base. Stroll around town sampling the musical pubs, the cute shopfronts, and baskets of flowers. Visit the newly revamped Westport House to learn about The Pirate Queen, Grace O Malley.

Westport House

View from Croagh Patrick

Glendalough

www.glendalough.ie

Possibly the most popular of the one-day trips from Dublin is a trip directly south of the city to the Wicklow Mountains in County Wicklow. The focal point of the Wicklow Mountains is the lake of Glendalough which has to be Ireland's most-beautiful lake... almost.

Glendalough, or the 'Valley of Two Lakes', is one of Ireland's most prominent monastic sites, nestled in the heart of the Wicklow Mountains National Park. The 6th-century Christian settlement was founded by St. Kevin and boasts the remains of this impressive monastic sites. Nicknamed "The Garden of Ireland", Wicklow is a nature-lover's paradise with its rolling 1meadows, vast lakes, and hillsides blanketed in purple heather, and it is right on the edge of Dublin city. Try stopping in Avoca for food and high-end crafts.

St. Kevin's Church

Galway City

www.galwaytourism.ie

Galway City is currently enduring a backlash as it has become increasingly more popular. It is now the Nashville of Ireland, where people head for a wild weekend of mad nightlife. And there is a reason for it. The town is simply amazing with fantastic pubs, shopping, and food. Right on the doorstep of Connemara, it is the perfect storm for a good time. I recommend a walking tour to take in the history and sourcing an early spot in one of the great pubs with live traditional music. If it is a peaceful evening of lazy music and dinner you want, Galway is not the town for you. If you want the "craic[5]", meeting complete strangers who become quick friends and end up singing with them, then Galway is for you.

Galway Streets

---

[5] Craic is the Gaelic word for a good time.

Let's Get Moving!

Day Trip 1 - Dingle Peninsula

While surrounded by the wild drama of the Atlantic, Dingle is vibrant, alive, and full of artistry–the human kind. Creativity abounds. Maybe it's what nature itself brings to the table that is manifested in the streets of every village. Weave through any village on the peninsula and find artists of every kind. I discovered that many of them, like me, came for a vacation but decided the draw was too great and they opted to stay.

It would be easy to just get to the Peninsula and not leave the town of Dingle itself. Bohemian at its heart but also easy going and genuinely friendly, the town gets a bit mad in the summer but even in the thick of it, the place has a laid back portside feel to it. Head out beyond the town and you'll find so much history and the famous Kerry coastline, with Atlantic waves, salty winds, what feels like treacherous cliffside, triangular rocks headed for the wide-open sky and green gulping waves crashing against the shore. Try the Gallarus Oratory, an Early Christian church overlooking the Smerwick Harbour. You'll find Coumeenoole Beach, with its views of the long abandoned Blasket Islands and the winding road to Dunquin Harbor which is so steep it must nearly be abseiled rather seen on a leisurely stroll. Inch Beach is as long and wide as you'll find where surfers abound. Moving inland, you'll discover Anascaul, home to Arctic explorer, Tom Creane, and Conor Pass, the highest mountain road in Ireland. This is much more than a day trip. Allow yourself a weekend.

Don't miss the Slea Head Drive, a spectacular road that weaves and twists around the coast from Dingle. As you near Dún Beag, you'll find the Fahan Beehive where you will see clochán, medieval stone houses, once home to monks. These odd beehive structures can be seen along the Slea Head Drive, and if they look like a movie set that's for a very good reason – the same beehive huts on Skellig Michael an island off the coast were featured as Luke Skywalker's domain in *Star Wars: The Last Jedi*. Quite the pied a terre, though the air conditioning left a lot to be desired and I am almost sure the Wi-Fi out there is terrible.

Coumeenoole is sandy, with pounding Atlantic waves and black rocks adding to the cinematic drama. You might recognize it from the David Lean movie, *Ryan's Daughter*.

Be warned that if you are not a confident driver, getting around the peninsula can be terrifying. The cliff roads in particular are narrow, with a steep drop and I should add that there is two-way traffic on these pencil thin roads.

Beehive Huts

Dunquin Harbor

Here are a few places that I love:

The Little Cheese Shop
www.thelittlecheeseshop.ie
(+353) 87 757 8672

The local cheeses here are
from farms just up the road.
The products are laced with
the faintness of seaweed and
salt from waves crashing on
the fields on which the sheep graze. Mark runs the shop and is the
most affable of hosts. He is a font of knowledge for all things dairy
and he likes to chat. By the time you leave you will feel like you
know him. There is also a nice little collection of wine to pair with
the cheese. Bring a few blocks back to the hotel with some
crackers and a cheeky bottle of something for a charmed night
without breaking the bank.

Murphy's Ice Cream
(+353) 66 915 2644
www.murphysicecream.ie

There may be cheaper ice
cream available, but you'll
find none better when
these talented ice cream
makers add a local touch.
My favorite flavor here is Gin. Made with botanicals from a local
Dingle distillery just up the road, the tang of gin on top of a cone
is just what you need to cool you down on a warm summer's day.

Louis Mulcahy

www.louisemulcahy.com

(+353) 66 915 6229

Further out on the peninsula (the edge of the world really), you will find Louis Mulcahy, a legendary potter (and Wexford native). Louis has built a gorgeous store with the most magnificent views you can see on the whole island. The pottery reflects the waves and plain life of the region. It is elegant and native, all at once.

Brian de Staic

(+353) 66 915 1298

www.briandestaic.com

This jewelry designer is world renowned and has been part of the national scene for decades. His designs are unique, pristine, and very clearly Irish. His work with the ancient language of Ogham is surely his calling card. You can get your name carved in Ogham on his signature pieces and you'll be delighted to see that they don't cost the earth. Situated on the west side of the town, it is worth the drive and as luck would have it, it is located just down the road from the Dingle Distillery. So...dessert anyone?

Dingle Benners Hotel

(+353) 66 915 1638

www.dinglebenners.com

Though an odd name for this family-friendly stay in the heart of Dingle, the Dingle Benners Hotel is walking distance to several pubs and restaurants and a 5-minute stroll to the harbor. I mentioned the place earlier, but I love the beautiful hotel bar and you will find plenty of parking, a major plus in the summer when spaces are few and far between. I found the service to be superb, giving its guests that family-run feel. The breakfast was a sedate, top-notch affair, and if you fancy a night out on the town, they offer in-room childcare. However, you really don't have to spend too much money on fancy restaurants as you can get fresh fish and chips right on Dingle harbor. I've tried nearly all the chippers and was impressed every time.

Inch Beach.

I can't talk about Dingle without mentioning Inch Beach. Its name may seem ironic since its sands expand for nearly 4 miles across the entire south-west side of the Inch Peninsula. On the dullest of grey days or on a blazing hot summer's day, it is breathtaking. I personally prefer it when it is miserable and empty. In the summer you will find surfboards for rental. You might not get a tan, but you will get the waves.

Inch Beach

Music

Dingle is not the stop for pipes and airs. It is the stuff of jigs, reels and polkas performed in a frenzy, to make you rejoice, smile, and even dance. This should reflect your choice of music while you are there.

My recommendation for Dingle is FLOOK (www.flook.co.uk). Flook is an Anglo-Irish band playing traditional-style instrumental music, much of it penned by the band themselves. No songs, mind you. This is frenetic stuff. Their music is extremely fast, ever percussive, with arguably the best bodhran (Irish drum) player in the world, flute and whistle atop complex guitar. Flook is made up of Brian Finnegan, Sarah Allen, Ed Boyd and John Joe Kelly. I am a mad fan. I've often said I want this playing during my funeral to keep everyone's feet tapping.

Day Trip 2 - Wicklow

Deity, Distillery & Demesne

Wicklow, just south of Dublin is not only perfect for a 3-hour drive just outside the city but also a full-on vacation. Wooded and mountainous with winding roads all leading to the Irish sea, Wicklow has a mystical air about it. Being honest, I came to the delights of "Wickleh" as we call it at home, late. I literally skipped the county on my way to Dublin. Over the past few years and with many of my tours, the county has unveiled itself. I am, time and time again, struck by its elegance. Its civility. There is a politeness to the place, which is probably another reason I avoided it for so long. Now I am making up for lost time.

Powerscourt House and Garden
www.powerscourt.com
(+353) 1 204 6000

My tours around Ireland take me to many grand estates but few match the grandeur and acreage of this estate in Enniskerry, Co, Wicklow, sa`q20 to 30 minutes to the South of Dublin. The enormous estate has two main access points, one at the main Powerscourt entrance and one serving Powerscourt Waterfall. (More on that later) The easiest way to get there is by car and there is a large, free parking lot on the site.

Day trips from Dublin are also available and they include entry fees to the gardens. The Powerscourt Estate extends over more than 1000 acres of land, 47 of them contain its beautiful and elegant gardens. The first landscape architects started work on this land in 1731 but it was only in the mid-1800s that the gardens took on the grand appearance for which they are globally known today. The result of many years of immaculate care is a stunning garden landscape which transforms into something new at every turn. The wide, formal terraces give the Estate its grand elegance but the aspect of the gardens, with the Sugar Loaf peak juxtaposed as a backdrop, makes them feel part of the surrounding landscape, almost a natural feature themselves, as if some deity with a degree in design had put it together. The formality blends seamlessly to the wild.

While the Italianate gardens grace the covers of all the brochures you read about the Estate and they are indeed an impressive sight, my personal favorites are the off-center walled spaces. I have never seen a more gorgeous walled rose garden. There is also a surprising neighbor of wildflowers and herbs. Wide terraces extend all the way up to the Sugar Loaf Mountain, the crisp green of the manicured lawns blend with the green of the mountain while showing off the purple heather. If you want elaborate fountains and sculptures, they are all there too.

There is a magnificent Japanese garden, hidden away and perfect for a calming moment or two in the middle of tourist season. Keep in mind that in the summer here gets a bit mad so plan your visit accordingly.

One of the reasons that kids love Powerscourt is a very special museum on the first floor of the main Powerscourt House, Tara's Palace. This museum is the home of the biggest doll's house in Ireland, and it is truly stunning. The house is protected by a glass case, so don't expect to play in it, but its many rooms are all beautifully furnished with period pieces and have incredibly detailed decorations including hand-painted ceilings. It's a wonder.

As for the big house itself, the very first building in the Powerscourt Estate was a castle dating back to medieval times. In 1730 the Viscount decided to redesign its property from scratch and transform it into an elegant Italianate villa. The house was completed in 1741 and had 68 rooms with beautiful furnishings that made its mark in the architectural world.

In 1974, however, tragedy struck when a fire broke out on its top floor and destroyed everything the house contained. All that was left were the original walls. The fire forced a complete refurbishment of the interiors of the house that now host posh Irish craft shops and a world class food hall. Eat your soup and sandwich at the windows to take in the breathtaking view — one of the greatest in the world.

Powerscourt Waterfall is over 350 feet tall and the highest in Ireland. While it is located inside the Powerscourt Estate, it is a long way from the main house and difficult to get to on foot. It is quite the walk and with so much to see on the Estate, you might want to think about taking an extra day for that trek.

Powerscourt Distillery
(+353) 1 506 5656
www.powerscourtdistillery.com

In the old mill house on the grounds, right beside the main house you will find the Powerscourt Distillery. Which boasts three extravagant pot stills, six separate tasting rooms, a gift shop, a café and a screening room. The Estate developed the 200-year-old cut-stone outhouses, barns and farm buildings and fused the old with the new with contemporary floor to ceiling windows. Tasteful to a fault.

The Distillery has the capacity to produce an annual output of one million litres of whiskey a year. Currently the team place about 100 casks a week in their purpose-built maturation warehouse. I sampled their wares in Season Two of the show and have to say I was very impressed. So impressed that I barely remember leaving! I highly recommended adding some adult tasting fun to your day trip. Just make sure someone else is driving.

Glendalough
www.glendalough.ie

Further south, in a glacial valley below the Wicklow Mountains, is one of our most important monastic sites in Ireland. The monastery was founded by St. Kevin in the 6th century and became known as the Monastic City. This is worth at least a few hours between the visitor center and walks around the site itself. The most impressive thing to see is the remarkably well-preserved, 90 feet tall Round Tower, headed straight for the sky like an ancient rocket ship. Near St. Mary's Church is the 12th-century Priest's House; a tall granite cross dating to the sixth or seventh century; and the largest church, which dates to the 11th and 12th centuries.

Near Glendalough are two cool historic sites: the 11th-century Trinity Church and St. Saviour's Priory, with Romanesque stone carvings. Information at the visitor center will help you find and identify the various landmarks, and you can also follow marked nature trails. Hiking boots are recommended. Between getting to the sites and the actual walking trails you will put in a few miles. In fact, many people go to Glendalough, just to walk.

If you're driving to Glendalough from Dublin, stop to admire the scenery of the Wicklow Mountains, including Wicklow Gap and the dramatic Turlogh Waterfall, and don't miss Louch Tay or the Guinness Lake (as it is called for obvious reasons). It also happens to be a scene used for the movie, *Braveheart*.

Avoca Mills Store and Café
www.avoca.com
(+353) 402 35105

In the village of Kilmacanogue, this is the perfect spot for lunch. I am mad about their gorgeous throws and blankets. They are scattered all over my house. I am also addicted to their menu. The salad selections alone are worth the trip.

Glendalough

Where to Stay in Wicklow

Brook Lodge & Macreddin Village
(+ 353) 402 36444
www.brooklodge.com

Macreddin Village features an assortment of superb accommodations from classic country-house style bedrooms through to state-of-the-art modern suites. The Village boasts the first certified Organic Restaurant in Ireland - The Strawberry Tree. I AM A MAD FAN.

Rathsallagh House
(+353) 45 403 112
www.rathsallagh.com

The O'Flynn family insists that this spot is not a hotel and I agree. The pace of life around the country house and gardens ensure that the atmosphere is kept decidedly slow...very slow. Rooms are elegantly furnished in classic Irish country-house style, with comfortable seating areas and open fires. Bedrooms, as in all old houses, do vary–so when booking a room, ask what is available. Some are more spacious than others. By the way, if you have kids with you, I suggest skipping this spot out of respect for fellow guests. It is simply too quiet for children.

The Music of Wicklow
Anuna is not only our greatest choral group but they've a huge influence on choral sounds globally. That sound created by their leader Michael McGlynn is a major theme of the singing sounds of Riverdance. Their Latin and old Irish acapella chants are just perfect for a prayerful stroll around the antiquities of a country estate or indeed a monastery. If you don't feel a connection to a higher being listening to this stuff, you are never going to feel it.

The sounds elevate, console, calm and inspire. Before you head into the site itself, I urge you to download some albums by Anuna. www.anuna.ie

Day Trip 3 - Wexford

Full disclosure: Before I start on my home county, it is important to acknowledge that I am biased, and this is a purely subjective view of the area. I must tread lightly for the sake of my friendships. That said, I will work my way around the county first, ending up in Wexford. I will also suggest www.visitwexford.ie which contains a lot of information and useful links.

National Heritage Park
www.irishheritage.ie

Right before the estuary of the Slaney River is a truly unique outdoor museum that journeys through 9,000 years of Irish history. The park holds about 14 hectares of natural forest and wet woodland, where you can walk by and through reproduced monuments. Among them are thatched Viking houses, crannogs (marsh houses), huts, stone circles, an early church, a massive Celtic cross and a ringfort made with the timber of 400 oak trees.

The walking trail is a trip back to Neolithic Ireland, and there are characters in period costume to add some context and more than that, a lot of fun. At the park you can build a house with wattle, shoot a Viking bow and pan for gold, while children can let off steam at two adventure playgrounds. There is also a fascinating falconry exhibit. The food in the restaurant is pretty fantastic, by the way.

Tintern Abbey
www.heritageireland.ie

Tintern Abbey is a former Cistercian monastery built at the top of the 13th century. The founder was William Marshal, 1st Earl of Pembroke, and a name that pops up in many parts of Ireland.

The abbey's monks came from the original Tintern Abbey in Wales and after the dissolution of monasteries, the property passed into the hands of the Colclough family who lived here right up to the 1960s. For this reason, Tintern Abbey has remains intact. Forty-five-minute guided tours are provided of the nave, chancel, cloisters, chapel, and the dramatic main tower.

Colclough Walled Garden
www.colcloughwalledgarden.com

Neighboring Tintern Abbey, the Colclough Walled Garden was planted in a green vale by the Colclough Baronets in the early-1800s. The compound is one hectare in size and divided into east and west sections by another wall. The east section is ornamental and made up of colorful borders, formal lawns and diamond-shaped flowerbeds, while the west is a kitchen garden growing herbs and vegetables. A slender river flows through the length of the garden and is crossed by five little bridges.

Johnstown Castle
www.johnstowncastle.ie

I spent my childhood circling the lake that graces the back of this Disneyesque castle. Recently refurbished and now finally getting the attention it deserves, Johnstown is truly a world to escape into. With acres of beautifully and naturally landscapes gardens, graceful pools of still dark water, peacock cries and romantic walkways this is truly of another time. You can also get inside the castle to see just how landed gentry lived. The 200-year-old farm buildings at contain a museum about the history of rural life in Ireland which I truly didn't think I would enjoy but I found fascinating.

The Irish Agricultural Museum was established in the 1970s and chronicles the many changes that the Industrial Revolution brought to farming in Ireland, when horses were overtaken by the combustion engine. The museum also digs into the harsh reality of the Great Hunger. You can look inside the different rooms that you'd find at a traditional farm, like a basket-maker, cooper, wheelwright, harness-maker and blacksmith.

There is a brand-new visitor center, restaurant and gift store.

Hook Head, Loftus, and a magical Maze.
www.hookheritage.ie

Hook Head is said to have found its way into common English usage in the saying "By Hook or by Crook." A phrase that came from a vow made by Oliver Cromwell to take Waterford by Hook (on the Wexford side of the estuary) or by Crook (a village on the Waterford side of the estuary).

Loftus Hall is a deserted large country house on the Hook peninsula, close to the lighthouse. Built on the site of the original Redmond Hall, it is said by locals to have been haunted by the devil and the ghost of a young woman. It has become internationally recognized as one of the most haunted houses in the world. It is also the place I my parents used to threaten me if I was bold as a child. Terrifying! It is about to become a 5-star resort hotel but I'm not sure how I feel about sleeping in that place.

The centuries have left their mark on the landscape of the Hook. From the majestic beauty of Tintern Abbey, to the 12th Century Dunbrody Abbey, one of the finest examples of a Cistercian Monastery in Ireland and on to perhaps the most famous landmark, the Hook Lighthouse; you will find a rich tapestry of unique and truly local history wherever you turn when visiting this unusual part of the world. A magical yew maze, made with over 1,500 yew trees and gravel paths, is a huge draw from kids and adults alike and right next door to Dunbrody. In Irish folklore, the yew tree symbolizes death and rebirth, so a maze symbolizing life's wandering journey adds some nuance to getting out of there as fast as possible.

Kilmore Quay
www.kilmorequaymarina.com

One of my favorite places in the world is Kilmore Quay, a small fishing village with lines of quaint to a fault, whitewashed cottages, and thatched roofs. Stroll along the marina and watch colorful boats bob in the water, take a trip to the uninhabited Saltee Islands to watch for gannets and puffins. Why not go on a scuba diving adventure or hire a fishing boat for excellent deep-sea fishing off the coast. Afterward stop for the freshest fish and chips at the Saltee chipper.

Wexford Town
www.visitwexford.ie

A narrow (read narrowest) artery of a street over a mile long with a north and south section, Wexford's Main Street is somewhere to shop, dine, people watch and go for a pint. Centered by the historic Bullring with a lovely little weekend open air market, many of the town's monuments are on or near Main Street, like Selskar Abbey, St Iberius' Church and the National Opera House but there are also ancient alleys from the Viking area leading down to the quayside.

WexWalks
(+353) 53 862 1 38062

Explore the worlds of medieval ports, bullrings, bloody insurrections, ghostly graveyards and cavernous churches. Hear about local characters, from monstrous murderers to vicious vikings to Oliver Cromwell himself. Join local actor and history buff, Paul Walsh, as he expertly weaves over 1000 years of history into one highly entertaining hour. He is funny and as Wexford as you get.

Selskar Abbey
Right in the middle of Wexford is a gem of an abbey that was established in the 12th century. Surrounded by a graveyard, the ruins of the Gothic church are in good condition considering the monastery was suppressed more than 450 years ago. Supposedly, Henry II passed Lent at this very place in 1172, as penance for the murder of Archbishop of Canterbury, Thomas Beckett. It is also surmised that the abbey's location was a Celtic monastery in the early Middle Ages. Sit in the courtyard beside it for an open-air coffee at Greenacres, an incredible restaurant, food hall and art gallery. You will also find the best wine store in the whole of Ireland (in my humble opinion).

Spice
(+353) 53 912 2011

Spice Indian Restaurant is beautifully decorated in a style that is both contemporary and warm, with rich, vivid colors. What is more inviting is the staff. Excellent, attentive service and just a feeling that you are so welcome. Dishes are prepared with the belief that Indian cuisine is not about heat but more about fine aromatic fresh herbs and spices. I am a mad fan of the mango curry here. They've also found lovely wines to pair with the spice. Ask for Emma and tell her I sent you.

Frank's Place 1860
(+353) 53 918 9109

This café/wine bar is right next to the Bull Ring on the Main Street. With outdoor and indoor seating, it is the place to see and be seen. A choice of a solid dinner menu or lighter fare and a fantastic wine menu make this place very popular. The staff is well trained, and the service will not disappoint. I love the coffee here and the scones even more.

10 West
(+353) 53 900 6883

New to the Wexford scene, 10 West is as much fun as it is tasty. The waitstaff is so eager for you to have a good time that you can feel the pride in their work. The food may not be innovative, but it leans into the local and pops with flavor. If you like a cocktail, this place does it better than anywhere in town.

Jaspers
www.crownquarter.com

Jaspers is the latest fun spot in town. An excellent menu created by local singer /chef /my first cousin Tony Carty. The menu features lots of locally sourced produce and they usually have sharing options. I recommend trying their cocktails. You wont want to miss the décor and the atmosphere.

Day Trip 4 – Tipperary (Tipp)

Tipperary Town or ("Tipp Town" as it is known) has a population of around 5,000 and gave its name to the county. Tipp Town was founded in the 13th century soon after the Norman/English invasion of Ireland.

There's a laid-back nature to the county of Tipperary and its people. I know you could arguably describe every county in that way, but I find Tipp people to take life handy. Stress isn't front and center with them, particularly if it would require breaking a sweat.

Heart of the hidden heartland, it has lush landscapes, ragged fortresses, mature woodlands, aimlessly wandering lakes touching many other counties, horses a plenty, and a different view around every corner.

Clonmel, Nenagh, Carrick on Suir, Cashel and Tipperary are the biggest towns of the county, the sixth largest of Ireland's 32 counties by area and completely landlocked. It has a diverse terrain with several mountain ranges including the Knockmealdown, the Galtee, the Arra Hills, and the Silvermine Mountains.

To me the town itself is a drive through kind of place on the road between Waterford and Limerick. In my college days in Limerick, we would drive out to Corny's pub in the town. Founded in the 1700s the place is the kind of pub where you are likely to find yourself talking to someone and even more likely to end up singing with them after a few jars. If truth be told, I've left that establishment many hours after I should have and quite often many hours after I was legally allowed to be in any pub.

Cahir Castle

Down the road from Tipp town is Cahir. Designed as a defensive location, Cahir Castle is an imposing structure that seems to grow out from the rock on which it stands. As you walk through the gate you will find yourself in the center of the fortress. Explore the castle which was captured just three times in its history. It still retains its impressive keep, tower and much of its original defensive structure. You can see just why invaders had a hard time getting in. Once inside, soak up the atmosphere with its maze-like hallways with winding stairs to wander. There is a great hall used for local concerts and you can hear all about the many movies shot within great walls including The Last Duel, The Green Knight and Excalibur. In 1961, the last Lord of Cahir died, and the castle was handed over to the State.

Be sure to view the Swiss Cottage up the road from the castle. A cottage orné – a fanciful realization of an idealized countryside cottage used for picnics, small soirees, fishing, and hunting parties. It was also a peaceful retreat for those who lived in the nearby big house.

Built in the early 1800s by Richard Butler, 1st Earl of Glengall, (you'll find a lot of Butlers round these parts) who, we believe, managed to persuade world-famous Regency architect John Nash to design it. It is a folly of another time but adorable and worth the stroll up from the castle.

The River Suir Blueway

The River Suir Blueway opened in 2019 and runs about 35 miles in an east-west direction from Carrick-on-Suir to Cahir via Clonmel. The route is made up of walking/cycling trails for 15 miles which runs from Carrick-on-Suir to Clonmel and a further 18 miles of waterway along the River Suir which can be travelled by canoe or kayak. You can enter the Suir at the Inch Field right beside Cahir

Castle, in Cahir Town. For more information on kayaking and cruises on the river go to www.exploretipperary.ie

Cahir Castle

Clonmel
I confess that I have overlooked Clonmel over the years and I can't quite figure out why. I have had many the good time there. The Gaelic Translation of Clonmel is Cluain Meala, the Honey Meadow. Stop by Old St Mary's Church. See the remains of the medieval walls that once protected the town and have a wander through the impressive ruins of the 18th century Carey's Castle.

Magners Cider
Founded in 1935, Magners is Ireland's oldest and most recognized cider brand and is still made in Clonmel, using apples taken from its own 150 acres of orchards. Magners still uses the same recipe created by founder William Magner in 1935. Made with juice from 17 varieties of apples, Magners is fermented with a proprietary yeast from the over 80-year-old original wooden vats and matures

for up to 18 months. It is repeatedly filtered to achieve a unique purity which explains why Magners or Bulmers as it called in Ireland, remains a firm favorite around the world. Honestly, I can't think of anything more refreshing than a cold bottle poured over a pint glass of ice in the thick of summer. Be careful though. A few of them and you could potentially miss either a day because of drunkenness or worse, another day because of the hangover (or so I've been told).

Carrick On Suir

On to Carrick On Suir, the smallest of the above towns mentioned. Carrick is a lovely riverside town at the other end of the Blueway with a bustling heart to it and some great little pubs. There is a unique singing tradition in the town, and I have spent many an evening there singing with friends. Carrick On Suir is home to the Clancy Brothers, the hugely successful Irish ballad band. They are arguably the greatest singing group that Ireland has ever produced with fans like Bob Dylan and Judy Collins in their heyday. My guess is you've heard or sung a Clancy Brother's tune if you've ever celebrated a St. Patrick's Day in the U.S. Download their albums and you will be singing along in no time.

Ormond Castle

Nestled into the fabric of the unassuming town is the best example of an Elizabethan manor house in Ireland, Ormond Castle built by the 10th Earl of Ormond in the 1560s. An architectural marvel, explore the two 15th century towers and country's only unfortified surviving since that period. Within its walls, you'll find incredible decorative plasterwork and a magnificent long gallery to explore. Tastefully restored and maintained by the Irish government, this spot isn't swarmed with tourists and manages to give you a glimpse of the past without any of the trite stereotypes. No leprechauns here!

The Glen of Aherlow

The Glen of Aherlow, Tipperary's scenic holiday destination, is a lush valley where the River Aherlow runs between the Galtee Mountains and the wooded ridge of Slievenamuck. Bounded by the rural villages of Bansha and Galbally, the Glen was historically an important pass between Limerick and Tipperary. Today there are opportunities for walking, rambling, horseriding, cycling and fishing.

Pilgrims travelled to Holy Cross Abbey near Thurles town for eight centuries to venerate the relic after which the abbey and surrounding villages are named – a piece of the True Cross of Christ's crucifixion.

Today this working parish church is a peaceful landmark and a place for quiet contemplation and historical discovery. As well as inspecting the relic of the cross, you can marvel at the building's everlasting stonework. The chancel is possibly the finest piece of fifteenth-century architecture in the country. The abbey also houses one of the only surviving medieval wall paintings in Ireland.

The Rock of Cashel

The crown jewel of the county has to be the Rock of Cashel. Perched on a mound for the whole county to behold, it possesses the most impressive collection of medieval buildings in Ireland including a round tower, a high cross, a chapel, a Gothic cathedral, an abbey, and more. It was once the seat of the kings of Munster and legend has it that St. Patrick himself came here to convert the heathen King Aenghus to Christianity.

The surviving medieval buildings today are as impressive as they were centuries ago and give the openness around the site. It is astonishing that they are as intact as they are. It is one of Ireland's wonders and in my opinion should not be missed on a trip to Ireland.

Many of the surviving buildings have stood since the 12th century: The Round Tower Is the oldest and tallest building on the site, dated at around 1100. The chapel of King Cormac Mac Carthaigh (MacCarthy) began prayers in 1127, boasting one of the best-preserved frescos of the period and the remarkable cathedral began in 1235.

Brú Ború
www.bruboru.ie

Brú Ború, (pronounced Brew Barew) located at the foot of the Rock of Cashel, is an affiliate of Comhaltas Ceoltóirí Éireann, the Irish cultural movement which has over 400 branches worldwide. The center promotes its cultural programme through education, research, publications, exhibitions, performances and information service. If you are staying in the area, I would heartily recommend their concerts. You will hear the finest of traditional music.

The Cashel Palace
www.cashelpalacehotel.ie

In truth, before this year, the Rock was the only reason to stay in Cashel. Now we have another.

I have stayed in many a fine hotel in Ireland. (Yes, I really do have the best job ever) However, the Cashel Palace has reset the clock for me. The Palace already had an excellent pedigree. It was built in 1730 for the Archbishop of Cashel, and is long open, hosting many pedigreed visitors from Lady Diana to Liz Taylor. However now in the hands of the Magnier family, owners of nearby Coolmore Stud and arguably the most influential people in horse racing, it has been transformed into one of the finest hotels in the world.

General manager and a gentleman if ever there were one, Adriaan Bartels hosted me recently and I was so taken with the elegance and the grandeur but more than anything the thoughtful, impeccable, and luxurious service. Refinement without being stuffy.

The breakfast room alone is worth the exorbitant price of a night at the manor. Everything from the local Ponaire coffee to the Strawberry & Champagne preserves all carefully, meticulously, curated to make your experience as unique and specific to the area.

The new wing adds to the original 20 bedrooms, while the gate lodge, schoolhouse and carriage house have all been restored, giving a total of 42 rooms, eight of which are suites. They are all individually and tastefully designed, free of anything that makes you uncomfortable. Think, Old Money.

Their services cater to their high-end clientele from a posh health club and helicopter pad to Equine concierge (Yes, I said Equine!).

The windows lead to the newly designed gardens which will need a few years to grow into themselves however they are anchored by the Mulberry trees originally planted in 1702 on the instructions of Queen Anne so you can rest assured that they will only get better. What a start! One of the Archbishops at Cashel was the godfather to Arthur Guinness, and a very early version of Guinness was brewed here. The cellar Guinness Bar honors this and the many celebrities who have stopped by (waiting for the nod. Ahem!).

The views of the Rock itself from the rear of the manor are remarkable, ever changing with the light and the half-light in all kinds of weather. As for the Rock and its posh neighbor, the Cashel Palace, they are now the posterchildren for the county, if not the country. When you visit the town, stop by the Palace, if only for a coffee and the much written about scones in the drawing room. Not for the budget conscience but worth every penny. When you're there, tell them that I'll be back soon. I'm saving for it, already.

Mikey Ryan's
www.mikeyryans.ie

If you find the Palace beyond your budget, I recommend Mikey Ryan's just outside the front gate and owned by the hotel. I very recently had one of the best meals of my life there. Tastefully decorated with low key but high-end service, the Mike Ryan's manages to hold it status as a local pub while serving Michelin-worthy food. After a spectacular meal I topped it off in the bar out front with a pint of Arthur.

Day Trip 5 – The Iveragh Peninsula

There are five peninsulas stretching into the Atlantic Ocean in the south-west of the country. The Iveragh Peninsula is one of Ireland's most scenic swathes of countryside, and a magnificent collision of mountain and ocean.

Between Killorglin and Kenmare, much of the heralded Ring of Kerry follows the rugged 60-mile meander of road around the peninsula's edge. Tour buses will linger in the center in nearby tourist hotspot Killarney; however, I suggest you look to the coast for something a little more out of the way.

From Killorglin, the ribboned road threads its way through coast bog and heather flecks dot the roadside which lies under the shadow of the MacGillycuddy Reeks which holds Carrigtouhil, Ireland's tallest mountain. This makes the spine of the outland. As you leave Kenmare on the Northern coast you'll spot Dingle to the north, which carries the weight of tourism, while you sneak off to somewhere just a little quieter.

Caherciveen
Built by the English in the 19th Century the old, barracks at the bridge in town was home to the Royal Irish Constabulary. This is a lovely, romantic, fairy-tale castle that looks like it was built for Walt Disney. It is steeped in history and, sadly, was destroyed by fire in 1922. It has since been beautifully restored.

Skellig Six 18 Distillery
www.skelligsix18distillery.ie

You might also want to stop by Skellig Six 18 Distillery. They offer fun and informative distillery tours where you will learn the delicate process of making Skellig Six 18's famous Artisan Pot Still Gin, as well as tasting sessions allowing you to try a variety of gins and whiskeys. If you aren't up for day drinking, I tried and tasted for you.

The Ring Forts

The Ring Forts just a mile outside the town are truly of national importance and one of my favorite historical sites to visit in Ireland. Leacanabuile and Cahergal both built somewhere around the 7th century are definitely worth a visit. If you have your wits and somewhat decent balance, climb to the top for some spectacular views and guaranteed bragging rights. (By the way, if like me you are afraid of heights, don't do it or have a shot of aforementioned Skellig Six 18 waiting for you at the bottom.)

Bray Head

A walk-up Bray Head will give you panoramic views and the otherworldly seaworn craggy pyramids of Skellig Michael and Skellig Beag and in the distance, Iveragh's star turn. Two lonely rocky outposts surrounded by the churning waters of the Atlantic, the Unesco World Heritage-listed Skellig Michael was first settled by Christian monks in the 6th century. It is a calf burning ascent from Blind Man's Cove up a flight of treacherous steps carved into the cliff face, the sky full of the resident kittiwakes. Skellig Beag, next door also supports one of the world's largest colonies of gannets. Skellig Michael's cluster of monastic buildings, beehive-shaped huts surrounded by the greenest of grassy slopes, a sense of a great being prevails.

Skellig Michael is now one of the country's star attractions. Star Wars filmed scenes on the location for the blockbuster movie "The Force Awakens" released in 2015. It was a very brief part of the episode VII Star Wars film, but they loved the natural and beautiful scenery so much they came back for the next installment, Star Wars film Episode VIII "The Last Jedi". I get it. Up close or from afar, the island is spectacular. For me I go by the recommendation from the distinguished writer George Bernard

Shaw who described the Skellig Islands as an 'incredible, impossible, mad place'.

Currently, visitors can usually visit the site from mid-May to late September. It is however a UNESCO World Heritage Site and has huge restrictions making it difficult to visit. Sailings from Portmagee are often cancelled due to the sea conditions, and you certainly need a head for heights when you get there. As of now, it is closed, and I suspect from now on they will make it more and more difficult to see it up close. It is a harrowing trip by boat unless you are an affirmed sailor and once you get there you have to climb the 600 steps to get to see the famous huts built by monks of old. I say watch from the shore. Either way, it will take your breath away.

Valentia Island
Beyond Caherciveen, one place the tour buses often miss is Valentia Island which played a huge role in the evolution of global communications. The world's longest transatlantic telegraph cable was laid to the island from Heart's Content, Newfoundland, in 1866 – the first permanent communications link between Europe and North America.

The island's main village, Knightstown, may be reached by a five-minute ferry ride from Reenard Point on the mainland and has an old-world charm that is well worth a visit. Before boarding that ferry, you will find one of my favorite holstelries, O Neill's The Point serving the freshest seafood and an incredible pint of Guinness. It gets crowded so watch for opening times. Still, well worth the wait.

Waterville
Waterville was the favorite holiday destination of Charlie Chaplin. He and his family used to stay in the Butler Arms Hotel. They first visited the town in 1959 and came back every year for over ten

years. There is a statue of him in the center of the village in his memory. At the recommendation of Walt Disney, he famously showed up but the staff, not recognizing him sent him away as he had no reservation. Someone in the lobby was clever enough to let the staff know who he was so they miraculously found a room for him. I love this wandering old hotel. The food and service are excellent here. I can't say I loved some of the room decor, but I found it overall a comfortable and comforting stay. The delightful dining room was a joy in the evening and the accompanying food was nothing short of excellent.

Kenmare

Ending the circle, Kenmare, is the unofficial last stop before the Beara Peninsula. Overlooking the Kenmare River, vibrant colored shop fronts line the three main streets, which were laid out in a triangle in the 17th century by its founder, Sir William Petty. Fast becoming the new foodie capital of Ireland. I suggest you try the pancakes at The Strawberry Field and for views with your dining, try the Boathouse Bistro at Drumquinna Manor.

Day Trip 6 – Kilkenny

I have a soft spot in my heart for this city. The birthplace of my father, as he reminds me often, Kilkenny has a life to it –a distinct personality: Quirky, alive, vibrant, almost funny. Although it is steeped in history it is very much looking forward.

Archrivals to my home county, Wexford, it has always been fun to give the city and county a hard time but there is also a smidgeon of jealousy in there. They've a lot going on.

Kilkenny Castle
I'd start with the anchor of the city, Kilkenny Castle. Few buildings in Ireland can boast a longer history of continuous occupation than this fortress. Founded soon after the Norman conquest of Ireland, the Castle has been rebuilt, extended and adapted to suit changing circumstances and uses over a period of 800 years.

Today, Kilkenny Castle is open to visitors all year round and is largely a Victorian remodeling of the thirteenth century defensive Castle. Each year, hundreds of thousands of visitors come to see this grand estate and walk through its fifty acres of rolling parkland with mature trees and an abundance of wildlife. Other features include a formal terraced rose garden, woodlands, and a man-made lake, which were added in the nineteenth century. There is also a tearoom, playground, and several orienteering trails for visitors to enjoy. All this aside, the singular reason to go there is to witness the magnificent Long Room and the art depicting the occupants of the castle over the years. If ever there was a walk-through history, it is here. I witnessed a concert-by-concert violinist Patrick Rafter here that will long stay with me.

Kilkenny Castle Hall

National Craft & Design Gallery
Across the road from the castle is the National Craft & Design Gallery. You'll find high end artists at work and displaying their craft. Kilkenny Design is where I usually end up spending a lot time and money. There you will find more commercial fare but not your usual kitsch souvenirs. It is a cut above the rest.

Tholsell on High Street and Medieval Mile Museum
Walk over to view the Tholsell on High Street. Built in 1761 to collect tolls it was also used as a customs house, a guildhall and as a courthouse. I would also sample the Medieval Mile Museum at the 13th century Saint Mary's. Displays of Kilkenny's civic treasures and replicas of some of the High Crosses of Ossory show the local Gaelic monastic heritage and the city's historic role in Ireland.

Michael on the streets of Kilkenny

Rothe House

Your next stop has to be Rothe House, a really unique Tudor merchant's house built in the 1590s. All of the above are within a 10-minute walk of each other so it makes for a tidy city tour.

Graignamanagh

For a break from the city itself I would take a drive out to Graignamanagh to stroll along the shores of the River Nore. Try stopping at Aran Bakery for a picnic. I love their stone baked breads and locally sourced fillers. www.arankilkenny.ie You can pick up bike rentals at Waterside Guesthouse. www.watersideguesthouse.ie

Inistiogue

You can also drive to Inistiogue which has to be one of Ireland's most pristine and picturesque villages. You may have seen 'Circle of Friends' the Hollywood movie, set there. It is tiny, clean as a whistle, still, and just perfect for that Instagram pic to stop people in their tracks.

Inistiogue

Jerpoint Abbey

Another sure fire stop near Thomastown is Jerpoint Abbey, an exquisitely preserved 12th century Cistercian enclave. The details of the scenes depicted in the stonework are incredible. There is a small but excellent exhibition space.

Jerpoint Abbey

Kilkenny City and Bridge

Pubs

One very important fact: Kilkenny had a reputation as Ireland's spot for stag and hen nights, so it got a bit rowdy for a while, however I believe that it has recently tamed a bit. The great thing is that you are spoiled for choice with the best of pubs. You are literally tripping over them.

You must try Kyteler's Inn. Established in 1324, the inn boasts of being one of the oldest in Ireland. It has a wandering olde-world feel with solid food and welcoming staff.

Kyteler's Inn

I would also try The Hole in the Wall, a tiny cozy pub that claims to be the oldest surviving townhouse in Ireland, as it was originally opened in 1582 under the name Archer Inner House.

For traditional music, I would try Andrew Ryan's is a much-loved pub that is regularly frequented by Kilkenny locals

As for hotels, I would opt for a couple in the heart of the city.

RIVER COURT HOTEL
www.rivercourthotel.com

The River Court on the banks of the Nore is 4 star and full of Irish vitality. Busy during tourist season it is right in the center of town so you can walk everywhere. Newly renovated with great food, the place might be a little too loud for the quieter visitors, but it has a lovely terrace to sit with a pint to unwind looking directly up at the castle. A spectacular view.

THE HIBERNIAN
www.kilkennyhibernianhotel.com

I also like the Hibernian, developed in an old bank and surrounded by the cobble-stone streets, it is old world but very, what I call, modern Irish. It is also just up the street from the entrance to the castle. I liked the upscale coffee machine in my room and the gorgeous city pub downstairs. The breakfast was also excellent.

BUTLER HOUSE
www.butler.ie

Built in 1770, Butler House is a luxury guesthouse. Formally known as the Dower House of Kilkenny Castle. This historic house is situated in the center of Kilkenny City, right beside Kilkenny Castle. An integral part of the Kilkenny Castle Estate, Butler House was home to the Earls of Ormonde, who also built the castle, stables, and coach houses at the rear. Sweeping staircases, magnificent, plastered ceilings and marble fireplaces are all features of this 18th century house. The house is a combination of contemporary furnishings and period elegance. I always feel far away from the city, within the walls.

Kilkenny Streets

Day Trip 7 – Sligo

If you are in Galway or Mayo, I would recommend a swift turn north toward Yeats country and the place to start that tour would be Sligo. Funnily enough, though is a world away from my hometown in the Southeast, it feels familiar. There's a lightness to it and at its heart is music.

Nestled between Mayo and Galway, Sligo is the second largest city in western Ireland, but it's not crowded or overrun by tourists like other towns. Surrounded by mountains and picturesque windblown countryside, the drive through County Sligo has some stunning scenery.

Sligo Abbey
Sligo Abbey was built in 1253, destroyed in 1414 by fire, ransacked in 1595 during the Nine Years' War, and pillaged during the Ulster Uprising of 1641. It has been through the mill but was restored in 1850 and remains open to the public. It is right in the middle of town.

Sligo Abbey

W.B. Yeats

W.B. Yeats, whose great work was continually inspired by the county, looms large. It's easy to see how Yeats loved Sligo and its surrounding pastoral views.

I will arise and go now, and go to Innisfree,
And a small cabin build there, of clay and wattles made;
Nine bean-rows will I have there, a hive for the honeybee,
And live alone in the bee-loud glade.

And I shall have some peace there, for peace comes dropping slow,
Dropping from the veils of the morning to where the cricket sings;
There midnight's all a glimmer, and noon a purple glow,
And evening full of the linnet's wings.

I will arise and go now, for always night and day
I hear lake water lapping with low sounds by the shore;
While I stand on the roadway, or on the pavements grey,
I hear it in the deep heart's core.

--W.B. Yeats

YEATS SOCIETY
www.yeatssociety.com

The Yeats Memorial Building is home to the Yeats Society. Every July, Sligo hosts the annual Yeats Festival with performances, music, exhibitions, and tours. We spent a wonderful morning in the center, learning of his life, his inspirations and best of all, reading his wonderful poetry aloud.

On the shores of Sligo Bay visit the recently restored Lissadell House and Gardens which has played a huge part in Ireland's recent history. The childhood home of Countess Markievicz, one of the leaders of the 1916 Rising, it was also a favorite place of the great Mr. Yeats. Spend a relaxing afternoon touring the house and check out the Alpine Garden.

At low tide, you can drive or walk across the 5km long causeway from Rosses Point and escape from it all at Coney Island. No, not that Coney Island. Keep an eye out for the rabbits that give the island its name. With sweeping sandy beaches, lush green fields and gentle hills, the island is a proper hidden treasure.

Carrowkeel
www.carrowkeel.com

You could also step back into Neolithic times with a visit to Carrowkeel. This collection of tombs is one of the largest and most important ancient sites in Ireland, with stone structures standing here for over 5,000 years. Visitors are welcome to explore, but please don't climb on or damage the tombs. It is incredible that people have to be told this, often.

Darty Range Flat Top
Head out of town into "the waters and the wild" toward Ben Bulben which dominates the county in his ominous presence. Part

of the Darty range this flat-topped wonder has a magical presence. Try not to gaze on the wonder as you drive by it.

For hikers If climbed by the north face, it is a hazardous climb. That side bears the brunt of the high winds and storms that come in from the Atlantic Ocean. However, if approached by the south side, it is an easy walk, since that side slopes very gently. The views are truly breathtaking.

Drive out north from Sligo town to Drumcliff to see the poet's grave. Buried here in 1939, he lies in an unassuming spot in a humbly marked grave reading "Cast a cold eye on life, on death, horseman, pass by." Penned by the author himself. For food nearby stop at the Yeats Tavern. Great locally sourced food and family-owned business.

Mullaghmore and Streedagh
If it's sight you want head for Mullaghmore, ravaged by the Atlantic the coast here has a Wuthering Heights feel to it. Head for Classiebawn Castle. Mullaghmore Head is a surfer's paradise if you are so inclined. Think full wetsuit though. Hawaii it is not.

Streedaugh

For a day at the beach, I recommend Streedagh. With historical features in every direction, you'll see where the Spanish Armada ran aground and can search for fossils in the rocks dotted along the mile long sandy stretch. It is easily one of the best beaches in the Northwest.

Classiebawn Castle
Classiebawn Castle is a 25-minute drive from Sligo town and privately owned. The castle is located on 3,000 acres of private land and you can't get close to it. However, there are wonderful photos to be taken with the castle lying against Ben Bulben in the background.

From here head into the amazing Gleniff Horseshoe and Benwiskin. The scenery is truly incredible. Expect a blustery day that will leave you wanting to head back to your hotel for a hot toddy.

The Coleman Irish Music Centre
www.colemanirishmusic.com

A trip to Sligo is also the name of a famous Irish traditional tune and to the learn about that I'd head to The Coleman Irish Music Centre, situated in Gurteen, Co. Sligo, is one of the best equipped Irish music centers of traditional Irish music in Ireland. It is dedicated to the memory of the legendary fiddle player Michael Coleman (1891-1945), universally acclaimed as one of the finest traditional fiddle players of his era. The Irish Music Centre which draws together the many strands of south Sligo's rich musical heritage was founded with the goal to preserve, promote, and foster Irish traditional music, culture, heritage, and the Irish language. The visitors' experience is informal, welcoming, and friendly with audio-visual presentations on the history of traditional Irish music, an exhibition area equipped with interactive touch screens featuring musicians old and new on various instruments, and an opportunity to even learn a step or two of a dance!

Where to stay in Sligo
www.markreecastle.ie

As for stays in Sligo, I was recently surprised and delighted with Markree Castle located in Collooney. It is the ancestral seat of the Cooper family, partially moated by the River Unshin and now a small family-run hotel. The stairs up to the grand reception lit with lanterns and twinkling candlelight will give you the shivers. It is truly magical. Sitting beside a blazing fire in the grand hall or the drawing rooms is other worldly. The 30 or so rooms are large and comfortable. The estate itself is huge. Dining is high end and worth it. This is one of my personal favorite stays.

The Music of Teada
There is no way I can send you to Sligo and not talk about Teada, one of my all-time favorite traditional bands, founded and led by Sligo fiddler Oisín Mac Diarmada. Téada first came together in 2001. They have since cemented themselves as leaders in their genre. They tour all over North America, every year. If you get the opportunity, be sure to see them. Their Irish Christmas in America tours are so enjoyable. Beautifully produced, their latest album "As the Days Brighten" is a thriller and features John C Reilly as a guest vocalist. Yes, THAT John C Reilly.

The Wild Atlantic Way

The Wild Atlantic Way deserves its own book and I know that no matter what I write, I won't do justice to the enormity and the beauty of this region. This is the world's longest defined coastal touring route. It embraces the wilderness of Ireland's west coast, from deserted islands to secret surfing bays, and is a trip that will stay with you for the rest of your life.

From the whirling windblown top of Malin Head in County Donegal to the sophisticated foody town in County Cork, the west of Ireland will be everything that you want it to be—with its craggy Atlantic-worn landscapes that strike your senses to its soft, pastoral, and quiet moments bathed in the deepest green you will ever see. Almost (but never quite) a cliché, this long and winding coast has inspired wanderers and adventurers, poets and painters, sculptors and sailors with a shore that is laced with dry-stone walls, thatched cottages, broken down or newly roofed, purple heather-laden mountains that roll down to empty beaches with 5000 miles of Atlantic bashing against it. From North to South, lies 1600 miles of ocean-battered coastline, truly terrifying sheer cliff faces, secluded white-coral beaches, technicolor green and sheep-spotted hillside pastures, surrounding tiny coastal towns ready to welcome you into a fire-lit pub for an evening of trad, pints, and the best seafood you will ever have. Lose yourself here, escape and explore all of it, whether you choose the major tourist attractions or the off-piste, you will love feeling like you are on the edge of the world.

County Galway

Let's start with pronunciation because I have spent most of my life correcting Americans on how to pronounce Galway. It is GAWL-WAY not GAL – WAY. The county is home to the world–

famous Claddagh (pronounced Cladda) ring and Connemara national park.

Anchored by Galway city, it is a vibrant youthful yet ancient place with a frenetic, electric, arts-centered heart. This town understands what it brings to the table and is tourist centric without losing its soul. Although it is a city, it feels like a town with a high-end culinary culture, as many festivals as you need, and a creative hub with world leaders in design and performance.

If you intend to make the city your anchor, you must plan ahead. May to September is high season and it is loaded with tourists. Hotel rooms, despite their abundance, are hard to secure without advance planning. There are plenty of options from hostels to 4-star luxury hotels and many of them in the very heart of the city making your stay a walkable one. Traffic and parking are very difficult, so I urge you to splurge here and get a place in city center, if you plan on submerging yourself in everything that Galway brings to the table.

Speaking of tables, this is also a place to think about reservations. While there are so many options for getting food at the last minute, I find that Galway is the one place where you will have to wait outside to get a table.

Now, what to do in Galway.

Connemara National Park
(+353) 95 41054
www.connemaranationalpark.ie

Covering 2,000 hectares of the mountainous Connemara countryside, this beautiful area is one of Ireland's five national parks. Two short sign-posted nature trails, which start at the Visitor Centre in Letterfrack, will give you views of Ballinakill

Harbour, Inishbofin and Inishark—small, scenic islands just off the coast. The exhibition at the Visitor Centre depicts various features of the park and includes an audio-visual presentation. Grounds are open year-round.

Aran Islands
www.aranislands.ie

The Aran Islands, rocky and remote off the west coast of Ireland, are not only pristinely preserved, from white sandy beaches to the jewel blue of the Atlantic Ocean, but also embedded with Celtic and Christian ruins, ancient stone walls, and forts which have stood the test of time and the harsh winds of the Atlantic. Take the long walk to Dún Aengus and marvel at the audacity of building a fort on top of a 300-foot cliff. I am terrified of heights and famously fainted on top of this great height above the world!

The people here still speak their dialect of the Gaelic language and fishing is a major industry as it has been for centuries, so stop off for fish and chips while you're here. Visitors also can discover how islanders made a precarious life for themselves in this isolated world off the mainland. Explore the boat-making tradition and do not leave without some Aran cable knitwear. If these sweaters keep islanders warm when the forces of nature can throw the worst of weather at them, then it'll keep you cozy back in the US.

Connemara Sheep

Inisoir – Aran Islands

Dún Aengus

Music to Play in Connemara

Whether you are strolling through Clifden town, standing on the harbour at Roundstone or hiking the fields of Carna, I recommend listening to some poetry, the musical kind. For me the greatest current Irish bard is Declan O Rourke. (www.declanorourke.com) His stories are like paintings, his lyrics alive and his voice has the weight that you want when surrounding yourself in the wild scape of Galway.

You might remember the Josh Groban song, Galileo. That song was written by Declan and perfectly frames his writing. Quirky and melodic with lyrics for days. Check out my favorite Irish song *Stars over Kinvara.* How I love this artist.

Declan has a new book entitled *The Pawnbroker's Reward.* Perhaps that should also be a buy while you are in the country.

Connemara Heritage Centre
(+353) 95 21808
www.connemaraheritage.com

> *"It's here I am today.*
> *God gave and took away.*
> *And left without a home for Dan O'Hara[...]"*

So begins the tragic ballad of Dan O'Hara, who lived on this site in the years before the famine and was evicted and forced to emigrate to New York, losing his family in the process. You will learn of Dan's story here. Connemara, crossed by the Twelve Bens mountains, is a stronghold of Irish cultural tradition and this heritage center remains a working farm with cattle, sheep, and world-famous ponies. You will learn how the people of Connemara survived from prehistory through the Potato Famine of 1845.

Kylemore Abbey
www.kylemoreabbey.com

While Connemara's wonder is most center, its natural sights, Kylemore Abbey is a standout exception. Buried at the base of a green mountain overlooking Pollacapall Lough, this fairytale castle has a romantic history and, a tragedy for an ending. Mitchell Henry and his wife fell in love with this spot on their honeymoon. He had the castle built in 1868 as a gift for his wife. Sadly, she died soon after, so he added a Neo-Gothic Church as a memorial. It became a Benedictine Abbey for a community of nuns in 1920 and they still inhabit this beautiful abbey-castle with rooms and gardens open for public tours.

The Sky Road

Truly a "Highway to Heaven", the Sky heads out from the beautiful village of Clifden on a seven-mile journey that is simply breathtaking. Be sure to take in the beautiful landscape with views from the D'Arcy Monument, Clifden Castle, the 1875 Coast Guard Station and the end-of-the-world experience of the Viking burial site of Eyrephort Peninsula before heading back to Clifden.

If romance is what you are after you will be well-rewarded here. This is not a place for quick drive through. It is a day to pack picnic and take in nature at its finest as you dine. It will undo years of stress. It will be a beautiful and peaceful day.

The Sky Road

County Limerick

Adare Heritage Centre
(+353) 61 385 186
www.adareheritagecentre.ie

In the heart of the exceptionally pretty village of Adare, the Adare Heritage Centre offers tours of Desmond castle, the standing ruins of a 13th century castle and fort in the depths of the turbulent late Middle Ages. The centre's tourist information office, coffee shop, woolens and craft shops make it an ideal coach-stop. Walking tours of Adare's thatch cottage-lined streets are also available from the centre or just stroll down the street yourself for that Instagram moment in front the cottages.

Lough Gur
www.loughgur.com

Lough Gur is the probably the most important Stone Age site in Ireland. The visitor center, on its lakeside site, contains a display and audio-visual show presenting the site's history. The archaeology of the area reflects the activities of the first farmers in the region, their dwellings, ritual and burial sites, as well as examples of tools and implements, The story stretches over 5,000 years back.

Glin Castle and Gardens
(+353) 87 329 4575
www.glin-castle.com

The FitzGerald's have lived here since the 1200s. It was here in the 14th century that the Earl of Desmond named his three illegitimate sons hereditary knights, White, Green, and Black. The last of these was given Glin and together the three Knights defended their land against the armies of Elizabeth I and throughout the plantation and penal years under Cromwell. There have been 29 Black Knights of Glin in total. The castle itself has a unique collection of 18th century furniture by Irish craftsmen. It is possible to stay overnight, and group dinners and lunches may be arranged. Formal gardens surround the castle with clipped hedges, urns and busts. A kitchen garden filled with vegetables, herbs, sweet peas and gnarled fruit trees is home to hens. Check out their gothic hen house.

King Johns Castle
(+ 353) 61 360 788
www.kingjohnscastle.com

King Johns Castle is at the heart of Limerick's medieval heritage area on Kings Island. Restored with displays and models, you can also enjoy a presentation of 800 years of Limerick history. The views of the River Shannon from the towers are worth admission, alone. The has been ongoing archaeological digs that have revealed pre-Norman houses.

County Clare
Admittedly I have a soft spot for this part of the world. The banner county as it is known holds some of the best nights of music and the greatest memories of my youth. Arguably it is the traditional music capital of the country and undeniably there are spots to catch on the west coast, but County Claire holds hidden treasures on the eastern border.

Cliffs of Moher
(+353) 65 708 6141
www.cliffsofmoher.ie

I've mentioned it before and will again. Just north of Lahinch on the coast of West Clare are the Cliffs of Moher. If you are looking for one of the Wonders of the World, here it is. Natural ramparts against the might of the Atlantic, rise to over 700 ft in places and stretch north for almost 5 miles. O'Brien's Tower, constructed in the early 19th century served as a viewing point for Victorian tourists and is located on the highest cliff. From that vantage point you can view the Clare coast, the

Aran Islands and mountains as distant as Kerry in the South and Connemara, up north. It will leave you breathless and wind worn. Follow this outing with a trip back down to Lahinch for a pint and bowl of warming soup.

Cliffs of Moher

The Burren National Park and Poulnabrone Dolmen

The Burren Centre and Kilfenora Cathedral
(+353) 65 682 7693
www.theburrencentre.ie
(+353) 65 708 8030
www.burrennationalpark.ie

The Burren National Park is an otherworldly landscape composed mostly of bare limestone. As you hop along the rocky road to reach the park you can imagine what it must feel like to walk on the moon. Yet life has found a way in this truly unique environment and all manner of wildflowers and greenery grow in patches in the cracks between the rock. It may seem an unlikely place for people to live and, indeed, flourish and yet it is here we find the oldest evidence of human activity on the island of Ireland. The Poulnabrone Dolmen is an enormous portal tomb erected on a high point in this barren landscape during the neolithic period, more than 5,000 years ago. It's truly a marvel and a mystery and not to be missed!

The Burren is indeed one of the strangest places on the planet. The rocky desert is also rich with life, and there's no better place to learn about it than the Burren Centre found in the charming village of Kilfenora. It's a lovely introduction not only to the flora and fauna found amongst the limestone but also to the way people have managed to live there for thousands of years. This landscape offers lessons in the geology and geography of the area, the rich diversity of Burren flora and fauna, and the history of man. A parlor is dedicated to the memorabilia of the Kilfenora Ceílí band, one of Ireland's oldest and certainly most renowned traditional band of musicians and complete legends in my eyes. You might remember that we met them in Season One of the Show. Next door is a thousand-year-old cathedral, once the seat of this region's bishop and home to three intricate High Crosses. These in my opinion are the highlights of the village.

Poulnabrone Dolmen

Bunratty Castle and Folk Park

(+353) 61 711222

www.bunrattycastle.ie

Of Irelands top visitor attractions, Bunratty Castle is the most complete and authentic medieval castle in the country. Is everything around it touristy? Yes. Is it worth it? Hell, YES! Built in 1425, it was faithfully restored in 1954 and has furnishings and tapestries to match. The Folk Park, set on 26 acres, recreates and authentic 19th century Ireland. The Park features include a recreated village street, eight farmhouses, a watermill, blacksmiths forge, pub and restaurant and a display of 19th century agricultural machinery. Medieval banquets are held nightly all year round at 5:30 and 8:45. Do yourself a favor and head to Durty Nellies. This gorgeously decorated pub was the focal point of many an outing in my college days. If you catch me with a sinister grin on my face while we're there, I will be remembering some of my college shenanigans. Oh, if those walls could talk!

Mountshannon

Located on the banks of Lough Derg, the quiet and beautiful East Clare village of Mountshannon is a place of peace with serene Lakeland views, offering visitors a chance for either solitude or adventure. Lough Derg is Ireland's third-largest lake and is home to an abundance of wildlife. Mountshannon is also home to a family of white-tailed sea eagles, so keep your eyes peeled for these rare creatures! The 50-acre island, Inis Cealtra, was once home to a monastery, and today holds the ruins of six churches, an early monastic cell and a cemetery. There is also an impressive round tower that can be seen from the mainland. You can also try your hand at paddle boarding or kayaking on the lake.

County Mayo

Westport House and Children's Zoo
(+353) 98 25430
www.westporthouse.ie

Season Two offers an all-inclusive access ticket to the many attractions in Westport House Country Estate. It is a destination for the whole family. Those interested in history can enjoy the graceful lines and period furnishings of the 17th century Westport House, designed by Richard Castle. The current house is built on top of an old tower house of Grace O'Malley aka. The Pirate Queen. The estate has activities for the whole family. It is lovely day out. It is resplendent.

Foxford Woollen Mills
(+353) 94 56756
www.foxfordwoollenmills.com

Step back in time to 1892 when Mother Agnes, an Irish Sister of Charity came to Foxford and set up the Woollen Mill. You can trace her real struggle to establish the mill. The Foxford Woollen Mills Visitor Centre also incorporates the Mill Shop, Olde Mill Restaurant, Jewelry Workshop, Wood crafting, Art Galleries and much more. Facilities include tourist information office, bureau de change, baby changing facilities and coach and car parking. There are tours in Irish, French, German and Italian and they run every 20 minutes. A sophisticated operation.

The Quiet Man Heritage Cottage
(+353) 94 954 6089
www.quietmanmuseum.com

Follow in the footsteps of John Wayne and Maureen O'Hara in this novel Quiet Man experience. Visit the filming locations of the 1952 movie and explore the cottage typical of 1920's Ireland. It's four poster bed, thatched roof, emerald green half door and whitewashed front combine to charm all those who visit it. Yes, it's a bit hokie but it really is very sweet. The area is beautiful and perfect for film enthusiasts or those looking for a romantic get-away. Hole up in one of the area's many cozy accommodations and enjoy this 50's classic before exploring the sites. If money is no object, I would book a room at the Ashford Castle, one of the most luxurious hotels in Ireland if not the world. You many need to remortgage your house to pay for a room but trust me—it is just spectacular. I had a great time people-watching what with all of the posh guests from all over the world, admiring the lush furnishings of my bedroom and dining the Franco – Irish restaurant. In hope I am lucky enough to stay again.

County Cork

Cork is the Texas of Ireland. It's the largest county and often called the Republic of Cork. The biggest county in Ireland, it is centered by Cork City, anchored on the east by the refined foodie culture of Kinsale and to the West by the wild beauty of Bantry. Cork is very much a state of mind.

The English Market

The Market was created in 1788 by the Protestant or "English" corporation that controlled the city at that time. Today it is hailed as one of Ireland's best and it has become a tourist destination and a world-renowned food emporium. From cheeses and olives, cured meats, and exotic fish to imported herbs and spices the market is now a mainstay if you love food.

The English Market

Blarney Castle
(+353) 21 438 5252
www.blarneycastle.ie

Blarney Castle is one of Ireland's oldest and most historic castles. An ancient stronghold of the McCarthy's, Lords of Muskerry, and one of the strongest fortresses in Munster, its walls are eighteen feet thick in places. The famous Blarney Stone is embedded in the Battlements. Climb up to kiss the stone and be bestowed with the gift of eloquence. However, I go to the Blarney Castle for the gardens. They boast a fine collection of Azaleas and Rhododendrons which add a wealth of color. In summer watch for the blaze of roses. On site visitors will find the Blarney Woolen Mills, a shopper's dream. I've spent and over-spent many a day here. You'll find everything from china to crystal. There is an exquisite lace department and extensive clothing options. The enormous restaurant is excellent. This is one of my favorite stops in the country.

The Blarney Castle

Jameson Distillery
www.jamesonwhiskey.com

About 15 miles east of Cork City is Midleton, the home of the Jameson distillery. On this tour you will come face-to-face with the world's largest pot still. Enjoy a premium whiskey tasting or draw and taste whiskey straight from the cask in their Maturation Warehouse. With Irish whiskey about to take over sales of scotch in the US, this place proves to be very popular.

Cork City Gaol
www.corkcitygaol.com

Despite its impressive appearance, this prison building housed 19th Century prisoners, often in wretched conditions. Furnished cells, lifelike characters, sound effects and excellent exhibitions allow the visitor to experience day to day life for prisoners and their dreaded gaolers. Incorporated in the Gaol is a spectacular sound and image presentation showing contrasting lifestyles in 19th Century Cork to help explain why some people turned to crime. Personal guided tours can be arranged on request.

Fota Wildlife Park
(+353) 21 481 2678
www.fotawildlife.ie

Fota Wildlife Park is about 10 miles from Cork on the Cobh Road and is one of the most modern wildlife parks in Europe. Established in the 80s with the primary aim of conservation, Fota has more than seventy species of exotic wildlife in open natural surroundings with no obvious barriers. As I've said, I am not a fan of zoos in general, but this place feels different. Giraffes, zebras, ostrich, and antelope roam together on 40 acres of grassland, much as they would in the African savannah. Monkeys swing through trees on a lake island, while kangaroos, macaws and lemurs have complete freedom of the park. Only the cheetahs have a conventional fence and I'm grateful for that. Fota is truly a sanctuary, for many of the species housed there are under serious threat in the wild.

The Mizen Head Signal Station Visitor Centre
www.mizenhead.ie

Ireland's most Southwesterly point, Mizen Head Signal Station is now open to the public for the first time since it was completed in 1910. The Mizen Vision Visitor Centre in the keeper's house, along with the engine room, famous suspension bridge high over the gorge, 99 steps and views up the south and west coasts combine with the exhilaration of the Atlantic and the rocks against it, to guarantee a unique experience. Mizen is Magical.

Kerry Rainbow

County Kerry

The most visited attractions in the Southwest of Ireland are centered around County Kerry and its commercial hub, Killarney. The famous 'Ring of Kerry' and the Dingle peninsulas are two of the most incredible drives you could ever wish to experience. Plan at least one day for each to allow yourself the freedom to stop frequently along the way. Tralee is the county capital and is often less crowded with tourists than Killarney which is about twenty miles away. No matter where you go, you will find a unique charm along with an equally rare accent that needs subtitles, even for we Irish from other counties.

Killarney National Park
(+353) 761 002 620
www.killarneynationalpark.ie

The three main lakes of Killarney occupy a broad valley stretching south between the mountains. The lakes and the mountains that surround them are all within the Killarney National Park. The Lower Lake is nearest the town, studded with islands and the grand ruins of Muckross Abbey and Ross Castle on its eastern shore. The Lower Lake is separated from the Middle Lake by the wooded peninsula of Muckross. At the tip of the Muckross Peninsula is the famous postcard picture that is Brickeen Bridge. Dinis Island is further on, abundant with sub-tropical vegetation and home to the breathtaking views of the 'Meeting of the Waters'. The views of the mountains change by the minute, no matter where you stay. The hue of light and the half-light on the hills in sunshine or in shadow is truly mesmerizing.

Killarney Castle

Siamsa Tíre
(+353) 66 712 3055
www.siamsatire.com

I heartily recommend an unsophisticated, natural evening in the heart of the city in the company of the musicians, singers, dancers and actors of Siamsa. A professional group of full-time performers give a vibrant picture of Ireland's folk heritage and culture. Together they "explore, protect, and develop" the traditional artforms while continuing to innovate in song, dance, music, and theatre. Many world class performers started in this hallowed spot and to watch this perpetuation of Irish culture, alive and vibrant, is a sight to behold. It makes me proud.

Blasket Islands
www.blasketislands.ie

The Blaskets are naked sandstone islands sprawled in the Atlantic, two miles beyond the westernmost tip of the peninsula. Ruined hermitages and forts stand on several of these islands, reminding us that they have been a constant for more than a thousand years until they were finally abandoned in 1954. As with most of the coastal areas, the marauding Vikings were here and may even have had bases in the area in the 9th and 10th centuries. Famous Irish author, Peig Sayers, is connected to the Blaskets and her widely translated work depicts the hard life carved out here during the final years of island life.

Numerous ferries operate passage to the islands and tours of the area. Ferries depart from Ventry, Dingle and Dunquin. Just know the waves can make this a wild ride and you will need to be physically fit for the journey. Call to book ahead.

The Blasket Centre
(+353) 66 915 444
www.blasket.ie

The state-of-the-art Blasket Centre, on the mainland in Dun Chaoin, celebrates the islanders and their unique literary achievements. It is dedicated to the native Irish language and celebrating Island life. Inside you will films depicting the real lives of the islanders with actual historic footage. There is a fantastic viewing area to take in the islands from the shore and to stroll the paths, reminding us just how harrowing island life must have been.

Kerry Museum
www.kerrymuseum.ie

The Kerry Museum is a very fine museum housing artifacts of archaeological interest as well as models and interactive exhibits depicting life from Kerry's past. Take a deep dive into the fire which ignited the Irish revolution or enter the museum's special exhibits area to explore the life and adventures of one of the most travelled explorers of the Antarctic, Tom Creane. The Medieval Experience is a unique exhibit in the Kerry Museum in which visitors are transported back in time to the Middle Ages - 1450 AD to be precise. Great for the kids.

Tralee Aqua Dome
www.aquadome.ie

If you have kids with you, this is a massive water world where they can run wild and just might give you a chance to relax! The Aqua Dome features a sky-high water slide, wave pool, lazy river, whirlpool, spas, raging rapids, falling rapids, play castle, children's slides and play area, The exclusive adults only suite features a Finnish and tropical sauna, steam room, plunge pool and relaxation area. Ahhhh!

Schull Planetarium
www.schullplanetarium.com

This planetarium is a spectacle in the truest sense of the word. Sitting under the hemispherical dome in a darkened auditorium, spectators can see an amazingly realistic and accurate reproduction of the star-studded night sky. The audience sees the heavens portrayed with such realism they feel they are sitting out of doors on the clearest of nights. Star shows are 45 minutes long.

Derrynane National Historic Park
www.derrynanehouse.ie

The ocean facing windswept village of Caherdaniel is ideal for stopping off into Derrynane, standing at the very tip of the Iveragh Peninsula in County Kerry. Derrynane House in its sheltered woodlands is the ancestral home of Daniel O'Connell, known in his time as The Liberator, the first great Irish nationalist leader. Today, 300 acres of the lands of Derrynane, together with Derrynane House, make up Derrynane National Historic Park

Muckross House and Garden
(+353) 64 663 0804
www.muckross-house.ie

Discover the magnificence of Muckross just as Queen Victoria did in 1861. More than 150 years after her visit much remains the same in this fine Victorian mansion, set in the spectacular scenery of Killarney National Park. The refined gardens are resplendent against the natural setting of the mountains and lakes of Killarney. Rolling grasslands lead on to an expanse of rhododendrons. Have a walk about the traditional 1930s farm from a time when electricity still had not reached the countryside.

Muckross House

The Skellig Experience
www.skelligsrock.com

As George Bernard Shaw said of the Skellig Michael, "[It is] the most fantastic and impossible rock in the world [...] an incredible, impossible, mad place". It is this that attracted movie makers to it as the shooting location for the *Star Wars* planet of Ahch-To. The striking early Christian monastery doubles as an ancient Jedi Temple. As a wildlife home it is a favorite to gannets and puffins alike

Skellig Michael

"NORN IRON"

Most people who ask me about travelling to Ireland have a different tone when they are interested in heading North. I'm not quite sure why they hesitate but they do. My guess is that they fear they will miscategorize the province of Ulster. I understand this because I used to do the same thing.

Growing up in the Southeast corner of Ireland in the 70s & 80s there was a mysticism about anywhere north of Dublin. Mentioning cities like Belfast, Newry or Derry just added to it. They were the names we heard on the nightly news along with other words like car bomb, checkpoints, shot, army, explosion etc. It's not a stretch that this uncertainty would carry over, long after the Troubles ended.

Let me be clear. The Troubles are over. Long over. It has been over 20 years since any serious sectarian violence has occurred in Northern Ireland. Indeed, as I have found first hand, Northern Ireland is finally being seen as it actually is.

"Norn Iron" (as people lovingly refer to it down south due to the extreme accent of its people), is one of my favorite parts of the world to visit. It offers something distinctly different: a coastline that matches anywhere in the world, the best of pubs, whiskey tasting, and incredible food experiences, topped off by friendly, chatty people. Sound familiar? It should. It's just like the south with a different accent and a very different history.

The Northern Irish accent has, along with just a few others in Ireland and the UK, been the focus of ridicule and or at the very least, misunderstanding. The broadest vowels are added to everything. They are also particularly fond of the letter R while they detest W which will sound like a Y. Confused? You will be. Accept it. Don't be embarrassed to ask a local to repeat what they've said only slower. They are used to it. I'm from the island and struggle so let it go and if, like many U.S. travelers, starting in Dublin you might be thinking of just taking the train up to Belfast for the day, don't bother. Save your trip for the next time you are in Ireland or give Northern Ireland the several days it deserves.

The Causeway Coast

The Causeway Coast on the Northern seashore is a seriously beautiful part of the world that requires way more than a drive by for a few quick photos while on a bus tour. Hikers will especially want to plan an adventure along the coastal paths that wind the way along a shore that transforms its landscape around every bend. The coast leaves me breathless every time I have been there...from the hike and the views.

The Causeway Coast is a journey of strident beauty all the along the water, stretching from the mouth of the Foyle River in the West to the Glendun River in the East. It spans an area less than 30 miles but packs in the drama, overlooking the North Atlantic Ocean not to mention the coast of Scotland and offers an idyllic seascape that seems somewhat fictional. There is a different kind of magic up there. If you want windswept romance, this is the place for you.

Myths abound, steeped in history with terrifying cliffs, white beaches and sandy trails, dunes, forests, headlands, rocks, ruins and ancient landforms that look like ruins. From Castlerock on the West to Ballycastle in the East, the coastal towns of the Causeway Coast offer respite on golf clubs with holes almost in the water, in traditional hotels with a leaning to the past, with family beach life and better, beach food. While I wouldn't expect constant sunshine, it feels like there is.

The Dark Hedges

The tourism renaissance of Northern Ireland has exploded either parallel to, or directly because of, the success of Game of Thrones. I think it was inevitable but certainly the wildly popular television series has helped the cause with much of the incredible scenes shot on location regularly around the region. So, if you want people-free photos of The Dark Hedges, you either must arrive very early before the bus tours or you spend some time there, simply waiting out the groups. And it is worth the wait, especially when the buzz of the crowds is gone. It's an incredibly peaceful spot to enjoy when there's nothing more than the sound of the crows eerily cawing and the occasional rustle of the wind through the cathedral of branches overhead.

This eerie trail was originally planted by the Stuart family around 1755 to show off to arriving guests on the approach to their Georgian mansion. They planted 150 beech trees along the drive to Gracehill House. My guess is they anticipated something more ordered, but the trees grew into a twisting, entangled snarling canopy of shadows and light.

The Dark Hedges

Dunluce Castle

Perched mercilessly on the ragged basalt cliffs, is Dunluce Castle, a now-ruined castle is very close to Giant's Causeway. It is as dramatically set if ever any castle was and even if you don't want to explore the grounds and ruined stone buildings that remain, it's worth the stop for the photo ops to the east of it. This was Castle Greyjoy to GOT fans and it has to be one of my favorite stops in all of Ireland.

The castle is precariously set on an outcrop with treacherous drops surrounding it and connected to the mainland by a little wooden bridge. It's said to have been built by the McQuillan family in early 1500s, who were the Lords at the time. The family held the castle for 50 years, until they lost it to the MacDonnell family in the Battle of Orla in 1565. The MacDonnell family still owns Dunluce Castle to this day.

There are many legends and ghost stories associated with the cliff-top castle. One is that the ghost of Lord McQuillan's daughter, Maeve Roe, haunts the tower. Sometime during the 55 years that the McQuillan family owned the castle, Lord McQuillan imprisoned his only daughter in the tower after she refused to marry Rory Og. Maeve Roe was in love with a fella named Reginald O'Cahan. One stormy night he helped Maeve Roe to escape the tower. They climbed down to the Mermaid's Cave a hundred feet below, where Reginald had stashed a rowboat. He furiously rowed against the crashing waves, but they lost their lives after being tossed like rag dolls among the rocks. As you look down and you can see how that happened, quite easily.

Another tale tells of the fateful day that the castle's kitchen collapsed and slid right down the side of the cliffs and into the Atlantic. The collapse supposedly took everything with it, including seven cooks. But one boy who had been sitting in a chair in a corner was spared. It is said this was the final straw for the owners, who then refused to live in the castle any longer. The tale can't be true, as the kitchen remains among the ruins to this very day.

The whole north wall of the residence building actually did collapse and fall into the sea in the 1900s. The castle is only a small fraction of the lost town of Dunluce, which was an intricate network of streets and buildings built by the MacDonnell family in 1600s.

Dunluce Castle

Bushmills Distillery

A trip to this area would not be complete without a stop at Bushmills. The distillery received its license to distill in 1608 from King James I and they have been at it ever since, thank the Lord. It is pretty much an open "secret" that their ultra-smooth single malt whiskey is the triple distillation in their unique copper stills, which gives Bushmills that distinctive flavor. As I've said, I am a late starter when it comes to whiskey, but I'm fairly determined to catch up with the rest of ye!

A tour of the distillery begins with a look inside one of the copper stills that has been cut in half to fully see just what it looks like. The 45-minute tour winds through the different buildings, each playing its part in the distilling process, from the arrival of the water from the spring of the St. Columb's to the malting of Irish barley and moving on to the various oak casks which gives unique flavors to the aging "uisce beatha" (gaelic words meaning water of life). It means that much to us.

The Bushmills tour ends with a tasting. I mean you'd feel cheated if it didn't. I got to taste 4 of them but I am not sure if that was because I'm a nice guy or the fact that I had a camera crew with me, at the time. Either way, I didn't object. Bushmills whiskey is aged for a minimum of five years. We tasted Bushmills Black Bush, which is aged in old Sherry casks. We also had a taste of the 10-year Bushmills Single Malt Whiskey which is aged for 10 years in bourbon season barrels. We were also permitted to select a final drink from the bar, which included several of their whiskeys as well as an option for a hot toddy or the Bushmills cocktail of the day. I love it straight up, and but my companions chose a cocktail or as they would suggest, a dropeen of water which lifts the flavor rather than dilute it.

Be sure to check their opening times to check the start time for the last tour of the day if you plan to visit in the afternoon and especially if you've done the Causeway and Dunluce (as that can really take up the whole day).

The gift shop onsite allows access without taking the Bushmills distillery tour and there is a good café/restaurant. The restaurant offers home cooked Irish comfort foods like Irish stew with soda bread and is a good option for a quick lunch. Unless you are after something unique (and pricey) I suggest that you wait until Duty Free at the airport. Dublin Duty Free has the largest offering of whiskey all in one convenient location. Nowhere rivals it.

Giant's Causeway

Just 3 miles east of Bushmills, is the Giant's Causeway. The result of an ancient volcanic fissure eruption and a UNESCO World Heritage site. it is truly a wonder of the world. Giant's Causeway is made up of about 40,000 basalt columns that are around 60 million years old. Most of the columns have five or six sides. But if you look closely, you'll find columns with four or even eight sides.

This landscape you see today would have looked much different 60 million years ago, and it was only about 15,000 years ago that the shoreline here was actually exposed when the last ice sheet melted. The thick layers of the ice age glazed down the basalt columns, leaving behind the boulders that almost seem to fit together as perfectly as a game of Tetris. This is as close to science as I am going to get. I much prefer the mythological explanations.

If you lean into science (unlike me) take an audio guide from the Giant's Causeway Visitor Center, it will give you the legends and the facts. I've always firmly believed that facts get in the way of a good time.

Legend has it the Giant's Causeway was built and partially destroyed in a battle between two giants, Ireland's Finn McCool and Scotland's Benandonner but a little-known version of the tale is that the Causeway was in fact built out of love. Finn built the Causeway for love rather than battle.

Finn had fallen in love with a Scottish maid. Sad that he couldn't get to her, he walked along the shore, skimming stones out across the sea. Seeing the splash they made, Finn suddenly thought of a plan – he would build a Causeway to see his love. He worked all day, and made good progress, extending the Causeway nearly halfway across the channel. Tired, he went home to rest, confident he would finish the job the next day. Unfortunately, his granny had other ideas. Afraid of losing him forever to Scotland, she used her magic to call up an enormous storm. The waves crashed against the partly built Causeway and the rocks were torn asunder. Finn awoke the next day to see his handiwork had disappeared. That didn't stop him however, and he began to build a new Causeway. Once again, the stones reached out into the ocean, but that night again, his work was ruined. Finn tried again and again. The harder he worked, the bigger the storms. Exhausted, he made one last attempt, building on through the night.

The storms rose up around Finn as he worked and at last, he reached the other side. But the harrowing journey was too much, even for a giant. Exhausted, he fell down and died in the arms of his darling.

Behind him the Causeway he had built slipped below the waves for a final time. Finn's Grandmother saw what happened. Horrified by what her own magic had done, she turned to stone. There she stands to this day.

If you visit the Giant's Causeway, look to the bay before the Little Causeway to the West of Port Granny Causeway and you can see the stooped figure of Granny frozen in stone heading up the Stookans headland.

Most of the tour buses that make their stop at the Giant's Causeway make a beeline for the Middle Cause, or what's known as the Honeycomb. This is just one of three promontories and has the very exact hexagons featured in many a tourist photograph. Travel on your own and you'll have time to explore the other formations that the tours usually skip.

It takes a little more scrambling along the rocks to get all the way out on the Grand Causeway, but this is the part stretching out into the sea towards Scotland. It really does feel like giants paved it just for you. And if you keep watch out to the sea, watch for a lot of dolphins.

There are four marked hiking trails at the Giant's Causeway and it's well worth completing the panoramic Red Trail, which links up with the Blue Trail for a loop of about a mile. At the very least, take the cliff top trail down to the Giant's Causeway from the Visitor Center for incredible views over the entire bay.

It is well worth staying in the area instead of coming out from Belfast to the Antrim coast for a day trip. You really should arrive at the Causeway before 11am to avoid the crowds. While there is plenty of space for everyone, it just makes for much better photographs with much less hassle.

Be warned that while you can easily walk the mile down the road to get to the causeway, your only option to get back is to walk that mile back...this time uphill, all the way. If you struggle with walking at all, I suggest you stay up at the top of the cliffs and admire the stunning views. If you squint you can just about see

Scottish coastland where Lagavullin and Laphroig scotch are made.

Still, seeing and walking on those hexagonal basalt stones is remarkable. You can almost feel the magic of Finn's Grandmother's swirling around you.

Giant's Causeway

The Hexagonal Stones

Derry

www.derrycitytours.com

My favorite stop in Northern Ireland is not of nature but of the historic walled city of Derry, also known as Londonderry depending on your leanings. Derry was founded in the 6th century as a monastery by Colmcille who arrived from in Donegal to help convert the occupants to Christianity.

Derry is the second biggest city in the north and is located in County Derry. It borders Donegal which has a huge influence on it. This city is often overlooked and extremely underrated for people visiting Ireland and I can't quite figure out why. There is a real character here, if any town in Ireland has it.

Its name comes from the Irish word *Daire* which means oak forest. Derry is the only remaining intact walled city in Ireland. The old city is walled on the west bank of the Foyle River and is spanned by two bridges, one for vehicles and the other the pedestrian bridge named the Peace Bridge.

Although Derry was originally an almost exclusively Protestant city, it has become increasingly Catholic over recent centuries, coming in around 70% Catholic now. From its walls, you can spot the Protestant and Catholic areas by the political artwork that blazes the walls of every area in the city.

While there is a wealth of things to do in the town, do not miss those Medieval Walls, the Bloody Sunday Memorial, The Derry Murals, Peace Bridge and of course the Derry Girls Mural. The town is a walking town even though you need solid calves as it is definitely hilly.

I would recommend signing on to Martin McCrossan tours. Martin was so loved that he has a memorial to his tourism services in the heart of the city. I toured with his vivacious and funny daughter, Charlene. She is a credit to her father and to the city. These tours are highly recommended.

The Walls

Derry City center is surrounded by ancient walls that were completed in 1619. The Derry Walls are 25 feet high and 27 feet thick. These are the only walls in Ireland to survive virtually intact today. The walk around the walls is about a mile and well worth it. The views from them capture the city and give you a better idea of its layout.

The Bloody Sunday Memorial

A simple granite obelisk is surrounded by a small cast iron fence and a plaque that explains the Bloody Sunday massacre that took place here in 1972.

This was a civil rights march that started out peaceful and ended up with 14 dead and many more wounded. British soldiers were essentially told to gun down innocent civilians, the majority of those killed and wounded were shot while running away from the soldiers, and others were shot trying to help the wounded. Army vehicles ran down protestors, others were hit with rubber bullets and even more beaten with batons.

Craft Village

www.derrycraftvillage.com

This is a lovely little haven in the center of Derry, which is a reconstruction of an 18th-century street and square. There is a central square that's canopied and provides a wonderful space for local performers and displays. Stop by the Cottage Craft Gallery and Coffee for their famous scones, deemed the best in Northern Ireland. I sampled a few and vouch for them.

Derry Girls Mural

The worldwide hit Netflix series *Derry Girls* has been any time travelling touchstone for a generation of Irish people that grew up during the Troubles. The reality of British Army checkpoints, bomb warnings and peace walls are all exposed in the show along with the Catholic nuns and schools attended. It also happens to be one of the funniest shows you could ever watch. Stop by for a photo op at the mural.

There are a lot of fantastic pubs, many with nightly music. I recommend heading for the Peadar O Donnells with excellent traditional music and packed with friendly locals or the Walled City Brewery if craft beer is more your thing.

For food, I enjoyed Browns Bonds Hill, high end, expensive and worth it www.brownsbondshill.com

For incredible reasonably priced Asian Street food, don't miss Mekong. (Love the place).

For food ideas go to www.legenderryfood.com

I should talk about the Derry/Londonderry naming issue. Nationalists favor Derry and Unionists use Londonderry. The name of the city was not contentious in the 1960s at the start of the Troubles, it was harnessed by Republicans to send the message that Ireland should be united and not under the control of Her Majesty.

The argument to change the official name from Londonderry to Derry has gone back and forth for years. Hopefully we will one day see a return to its original Irish name. Nobody in the South would dream of using London anything to describe a place on the island of Ireland.

White Park Bay

Perhaps most surprising about Northern Ireland and the Giant's Causeway Coastal Route are the miles of white sand beaches that are fringed with water so blue you'd almost think it's the Caribbean. Almost – if it weren't for the wind, rain and cooler northern temperatures to remind you that you're really in Norn Iron.

White Park Bay is one of those incredible beaches. It's a 3-mile-long stretch of white sand set in a bay. Sheep and cows graze on both the hillside leading down to the beach. The beach itself making it look straight from a movie set.

Carrick-a-Rede Rope Bridge

The Causeway Coast has a long history of Atlantic salmon fishing with fishing the main industry in the villages like Portrush, Ballycastle and Portstewart for centuries. But it wasn't until 1750s when salmon fisherman erected the first rope bridge at Carrick-a-Rede that the spawning salmon were accessible.

A little island sat just about 60 feet off the mainland. The Atlantic waters that separate the island from the mainland were a course for the spawning salmon returning to rivers year after year. It doesn't sound or look like a great distance, but reaching the little island was dangerous in the rough waters between the two.

Salmon fisherman built a rope bridge spanning the 60 feet chasm between the mainland and the little island. It was a solution that made them less reliant on boats and finally able to fish the salmon from this spot. It's thought that the island itself, named Carrick-a-Rede Island, was named around the same time as that first bridge.

Salmon fishing continued right up until 2002 but it was stopped at Carrick-a-Rede because of the decline of Atlantic salmon from over-fishing in the ocean and river pollution.

The bridge we still see today was built and opened to the public in 2008.

It's located just nine miles down the coast from Giant's Causeway. The rope bridge sits a hundred feet or so, above the Atlantic. When it's windy, which it's pretty much guaranteed to be since it is Ireland, after all, the bridge sways with the wind. Though no injuries or accidents have ever been recorded at Carrick-a-Rede rope bridge, it's often listed among the world's scariest bridges and I endorse that. I have some cheek writing about the bridge when I have never, nor will I ever cross it, in my life.

Some tourists have been so paralyzed by fear of returning back across the bridge that they've had to be taken off the island by boat. I have no fear…because I will never put myself through it. But please – enjoy yourself.

Carrick-a-Rede Rope Bridge

Belfast
www.city-sightseeing.com

Belfast deserves a whole chapter, really but because I've so much to write we will give it a quick tour around. Belfast was essentially flattened in the Blitz. One of 16 cities in the UK to suffer the German air raids of WWII, Belfast was not ready for it and never believed the bombers could reach the city. Left with wide-spread devastation, the city, its shipyard, and its industry were annihilated. Then, after a brief respite, came that period from the 1960s until 1998 known as The Troubles when car bombings, rioting, shooting, and looting were the daily norm. Belfast has been through the mill. Is the town the most beautiful in the world? No. But it has so much individuality that it surely is well worth a look. Today, Belfast is a mix of modern architecture laced with the occasional historic building that managed to survive.

The drawing offices at Harland and Wolfe, housed the draftsmen who designed the Titanic and a wealth of major ships. They have been transformed into the rather gorgeous Titanic Hotel blending art deco with a nautical theme. It is a subtle design that is relaxed with beautifully appointed large rooms. The vaulted bar with its glazed ceiling is a particular favorite of mine.

A great way to see Belfast is the City Sightseeing Belfast hop-on, hop-off open-top bus tour (£18 adult, £11 child).

Belfast is unrecognizable from the city I knew from bad news on my TV in the 80s. It is now much livelier, buzzing, and almost electric, with much more diversity. It is also down to earth and devoid of pretentiousness. It is what it is.

I am a mad fan of the Crown Liquor Saloon, a Victorian bar which John Betjeman called "a many-coloured cavern" opposite the

Europa Hotel. The Botanic Gardens are a green haven for a bit of relaxation, with a magnificent Palm House. Next door, the recently refurbished Ulster Museum is well worth a trip.

St. George's Market
Start the day at the oldest continually operating covered market on the island of Ireland where you will find over 200 stalls to peruse.

There has been a market at St. George's since 1604, though the Victorian building we see today was built in the late 1800s.

It is open on Friday, Saturday and Sunday and the market changes each day. You can get everything from secondhand books to as much fish as you want. Chowder Up is one of the popular stalls with a line of customers waiting to purchase a cup of chowder. Highly recommended.

The Saturday City Food and Garden Market turns into a food fair from around the world with everything from local Irish breakfast baps and soda bread to smoothies and Cubans (the sandwich, not the cigar). There are vendors selling spices, chilis, cheeses and chocolates, as well as artists selling paintings, crafts, jewelry, and plants.

Titanic Museum Belfast
www.titanicbelfast.com

Back in the day, Belfast had the largest shipyard in the world and its shipbuilding industry made it famous. The Titanic, and its sister ships the Olympic and Britannic, were the largest ocean liners in the world at the time that they were built at the Harland and Wolff shipyard in Belfast. Since the day the ship launched, a day that it is said the entire city celebrated after the massive feat of launching the world's largest ocean liner, Belfast and the Titanic have been synonymous.

Opened in 2012, the Titanic Belfast is an interactive visitor experience that aims to tell the intertwined story of Belfast and the ill-fated ship. They do it very well.

While we all know the story of Titanic and her sinking on April 15, 1912, thanks in large part to Leonardio DiCaprio, Titanic is a ship that has long enthralled us all. With many other Titanic museums and a decade of analyzing the ship and that fateful night, what more of the story could possibly be left to tell? Quite a bit, actually.

The Exhibition begins with Belfast's commercial life when linen, not shipbuilding, dominated the industry in the city. Known as Linenopolis, Belfast was the greatest linen producer in the world, and this led to developing its port. Harland and Wolff launched their shipyard in 1858, and quickly became Belfast's leading shipyard.

The museum also celebrates the many achievements of Harland and Wolfe. As you move from room to room in the museum, you are introduced to the team who dreamed up the world's most luxurious ship. The pride to take on the project of building Titanic is evident in the detailed exhibition illustrating the technical design of the ship. Even the technical stuff is fascinating. Titanic Museum Belfast balances information and entertainment, quite well.

While there are no actual surviving objects from Titanic on display, there are recreations of a lifeboat and of the first-, second-, and third-class cabins. And as you wander into another room, multimedia displays show video clips of the launch day, and a floor to ceiling wall of glass looks over the very spot where

Titanic was built and launched on May 31, 1911. The exhibit remembers and honors those who died, with back stories and "interviews" continuing to address the actions taken by the White Star Line after the disaster. The exhibition ends with a short movie taking you 12,500 feet below the surface to where the Titanic rests on the ocean floor.

Even the building itself is designed to tower at the exact height that Titanic stood, giving you the perspective of just how large the ship was. From the right angles, the four corners represent Titanic's bow. And taking in the entire building, it could resemble the iceberg that brought Titanic down. It is a marvel of a design. It would be completely worth your while to allow at least 2 hours to Titanic Museum Belfast.

The Titanic Museum

The Crosskeys Inn
www.crosskeys-inn.com

The Crosskeys Inn in Tooembridge, County Antrim is the oldest thatched pub in Ireland. Sound touristy? Well, it is a bit but worth the drive out to it. Buried off a main road in the middle of nowhere the inn is like something out of a movie set, except it is real. Renowned for its traditional music, Crosskeys Inn is a unique, authentic Irish traditional pub if ever there was one. A turf fire in every room, the atmosphere as cozy as you could want. A stone-built cottage, it was once a coaching stop on the route between Belfast and Derry. (it's about a half hour drive from Belfast) The building until recently was thought to have dated back to the 1740's but in 2010 Queens University Belfast completed the dating process confirming that the building was much older, in fact dating back to pre-1654. You are assured a warm welcome and as touring around at your leisure is thirsty work.

The Crosskeys Inn

My Castles

If you've watched my show, you will know that I love a castle. The history, the intrigue, the drama, the drapes...all add to a fantasy life. I am not quite sure just how luxurious life was in the original versions of our great castles. Opulent, yes, but there always seems to be a story involving backstabbing, war mongering or skullduggery not to mention the lack of central heating or plumbing.

I, however, lean into what castles have become: lush estates, five-star accommodation, newly added swimming pools, spas, and, of course, Michelin star restaurants. In this case, I prefer to soak in the luxury rather than the history. To preserve these great architectural feats, I wonder at the families who have not only saved but nurtured a new path for these estates to not only survive but to thrive.

To do this, sometimes they must bring in big business from the hospitality industry and invariably it involves tens of millions of dollars. Luckily this seems to work. With a respectful nod to the past, if these companies can get it right, they can cement the past while elevating it to look to the future. I marvel at the respect but also the vision.

That is not to say I need all of this to enjoy a stay at a castle estate. There are plenty of options to match your budget should you fancy a night or two of pretending you are Lord or Lady Muckety Muck.

I'd like to give you my list of fancy houses, manors, and castles. Yes, I call them my castles. I plan on adding several more next season once I have personally vetted them. Somebody's got to do it, right?

The Flagship – Ashford Castle
www.ashfordcastle.com

In Ireland, it's not unusual for hotels to call themselves castles without being truly deserving of the word. You'll find a lot of "castle adjacent" properties around the country. Ashford Castle is not one of these hotels. The stately property on Lough Corrib is as castle as you get, from the unending manicured lawns to the turrets, to the never-ending hallways and paneling, to the gorgeous resident Irish wolfhounds who patrol the lobby in the morning.

Ashford Castle has a rich history as you would expect. The Norman, de Burgo family first built a castle here in 1228, and then lost it to the he 16th century. Like many other castles, it changed ownership many times over the following centuries and the building went through several renovations, getting the addition of a French-style chateau in 1715 and a couple of Victorian wings in the mid-19th century, before evolving into the hotel it is today. For 60 years, it was the family residence of the Guinness Family. The castle grounds were also used as a primary filming location for the classic 1952 film "The Quiet Man," which is a point of local pride (there is even a "Quiet Man" museum in Cong and a lovely, renovated building from the shoot on the grounds). Guests can watch the film for free in the luxurious, most incredible 32-seat movie theater. Ashford Castle is must-see.

The castle was purchased by the Red Carnation Hotel Group in 2013, and they gave it $75 million makeover that is nothing short of breathtaking

The lobby, drawing room, and Oak Hall have rich wood paneling; oil paintings, chandeliers, and fireplaces which can also be found throughout, and stunning views of the lake can be enjoyed from many rooms.

While everything looks gorgeous, it also looks expensive. I love it but feel somewhat undeserving. While there I was genuinely waiting for someone to ask me to leave because I reduced the tone...which I did. It is proudly stuffy. Everything from the curtains to the linens are top shelf. This said, I love it. The staff is stellar and welcoming. The training here is second to none. The comfort and attention to detail is faultless.

At dinner, jackets are required in George V Dining Room, and doormen wear top hats. It is part of the fun of the experience for some, but others may find it too uptight for their tastes. I am all in, dress up when I'm there and absolutely love it.

Ashford Castle

Dungeon Bistro

If you prefer something more relaxed, the Dungeon Bistro offers a less formal atmosphere. Watch for the wall of fame. Don't be surprised if you see Hollywood royalty having a pint opposite you.

Although the Dungeon is massive, there are only 82 rooms, which allows for a detailed level of service. Have I mentioned the truly impeccable service.

One of my all-time favorite Irish experiences is having tea and scones in the drawing room, reading the Irish Times and listening to renowned harpist Annette Griffin play elegant Irish airs. As posh or posh adjacent as I will ever achieve.

The Dungeon Dining Room – Ashford Castle

Cabra Castle
www.cabracastle.com

Cabra Castle Hotel is about one hour from Dublin City, near the town of Kingscourt Co. Cavan, and bordering the counties of Meath and Monaghan. Located on Dun A Ri Forest Park, covering nearly 600 acres as well as being a place of great natural beauty.

Within the park there is Cromwell's Bridge which, though dating back to the first Norman conquest of Ireland, was named as such because Cromwell himself, had crossed the bridge on his way to defeat the O'Reillys, the original owners of the Cabra Estate.

There are also the ruins of Fleming's Castle in Dun A Ree, which records show was constructed in 1607 by a Gerald Fleming, and another from the 12th century owned by the famous Hugh De Lacy.

As for the castle itself, it is imposing as you drive up the gorgeous winding drive. This castle isn't as pristine or as highbrow as Ashford. It is also about half the price to stay there so this may be a more affordable option. I stayed in a courtyard room at the back of the castle which was basic but comfortably appointed.

I wandered the castle alone and found stately, somewhat dusty rooms with massive paintings of previous owners who seemed to know I was staying and were ok with it. There have been, by the way, many reports of ghosts in this place.

I absolutely loved the food here having an amazing dinner at the beautifully appointed floral Courtyard Restaurant and one of the cosiest pubs next door, the Derby Bar. Formal yet comfortable.

It is open to the public during the day if you want to pop in for lunch to look around and perhaps enjoy on old world pint.

There is a lovely terrace looking out across the lawns. Though the design does not quite seem to fit in with the rest of the castle, it was lovely to watch the wolfhounds play on the green as I sipped a pint of cider in the sunshine.

The grounds contain tennis courts outside and a 9-hole golf course, along with plenty of paths and nature trails that lead on into the Dun A Ri Forest Park. I loved strolling without seeing one other person, losing myself in the woods.

Is Cabra, luxurious? No. It does however give you an elegant stay and a glimpse into gentrified life without paying an exorbitant amount of money. Watch out for that ghost though.

Cabra Castle

Cabra Castle Dining Room

Castle Leslie

www.castleleslie.com

Arriving at Castle Leslie Estate in the idyllic village of Glaslough you are teased with a gated entrance that makes you feel like you are entering another world. As you drive up the winding driveway passing the church, the anticipation is very real but turning the corner and expecting what Americans may think of as a castle, would not be a great idea. It is gothic manor rather than castle. There are no buttresses or battlements. However, Leslie is truly one of the last great Irish estates, dating back to the 1660s and remains in the hands of its founding family–the Leslie family – who returned it to its former glory from a crumbling ancestral pile in the 90s and who still live in the house. The main country house was built in 1870 on the site of the original castle and fashioned in the Scottish Baronial style. At first glance, it really does feel Scottish. Inside, the house exudes genuine charm and grandeur complete with personal hunting trophies, log fires, and family oil paintings and heirlooms. All the rooms look out on to 1,000-acre grounds with a picturesque lake front and center. Leading from the main house are additions including an elegant marquee for weddings. Just inside the entrance is a charming Virginia creeper-clad building that holds the Lodge rooms and an incredible restaurant. St. Salvator's Church is where Paul McCartney and Heather Mills famously married in 2002. Guests here are almost exclusively couples, as the hotel has a classically romantic atmosphere, though families find their way here as well. I was alone (as usual) and was moved from the top suite to the neighboring room as a hugely famous Canadian artist decided last minute to stay and she wanted space for her family. I won't name names but are almost guaranteed to spy a celebrity at Castle Leslie.

There is also the option to stay in the lodge down from the castle, with gorgeously appointed modern rooms, a fantastic bar and a restaurant that is upscale but casual. I had one of the best Irish meals of my life there during my stay. Treated to an 8-course tasting menu, I have a pretty good idea of the whole menu. They offer a wonderful, fixed price menu that is truly top notch and somewhat reasonable. I marveled at the overstuffed wine menu and the service that night should be the envy of Ireland. Impeccable. I will be back, again and again.

Castle Leslie

Johnstown Castle
www.johnstowncastle.ie

You will recognize the name from Season One as it the castle I grew up on...not in. I spent my youth on the grounds about 2 miles from my house. We would walk out in the summer to play around the arcadian walkways of the lake in front of this Disneyesque other world.

Johnstown Castle Estate has been home to two prominent Wexford families. The Castle was built by the Esmonde family who settled in Co Wexford in 1169. During the Cromwellian period of 1640s the estate was confiscated and changed hands several times. It was then acquired by the Grogan family in 1692 who developed the castle, grounds, lakes and estate that you see today and whose descendants remained at Johnstown until 1945. The property was presented as a gift to the Irish Nation in 1945.

It holds historic treasures inside the castle that give a glimpse into gentry life. I wholeheartedly recommend the guided tour before heading to enjoy the estate overflowing with trees and plants from around the globe, a lake path that will remove the stresses of any tortured soul, an excellent agricultural museum that in truth I thought I would run through but stayed and loved, and finally a modern restaurant and tourist stop to cater to the thousands who now come to witness the magic. While you can't stay, this might be a less expensive alternative to gain insight into five-star castle life. Don't miss it.

Johnstown Castle

Lough Rynn
www.loughrynn.ie

Set in a 19th-century castle on 300 acres sidelining the shores of Lough Rynn, this upscale hotel with separate self-catering cottages is a mile outside of Mohill, County Leitrim

The elegant, luxurious rooms feature antique furniture that lean to the luxurious rather than the medieval. Suites add 4-poster beds and free-standing tubs. Posh self-catering cottages have all modern conveniences.

There is a traditional fine-dining restaurant, that combines relaxed service with upscale but not uptight food. There is also swanky cocktail bar and a piano room. Afternoon tea in the drawing room overlooking the lake is gorgeous or sit by the enormous fireplace with an Irish coffee. It makes for a relaxing stay.

The grounds and walled gardens are a no-brainer. Take a long lingering stroll, ending in the bar.

I stayed in a very lush suite complete with a jacuzzi that would fit half of Leitrim. Standard rooms are of a high caliber and have many of the same period features as the pricier options. Set in the converted stables, they overlook a beautiful courtyard and have ornate stone archways above the doors. Rooms in the old house are plush and timeless. Either are just lovely.

My film crew and I enjoyed a spectacular night in one of their private dining rooms. Many people use this timeless spot for weddings. If you are flexible, I would suggest a midweek stay to avoid the crowds.

I loved the breakfasts here with exquisite additions like whiskey laced porridge. (Yes, I did!)

Lough Rynn

My Hotels

How do I pick a hotel for you? Well, I won't. All I can do is tell you places where I had a lovely experience. Some are five-star, some much less, a few famous spots and one or two brand new to the game, hoping to make their mark. The only thing linking them all is that they have managed to make me feel totally at home.

How do I rate them? Well, my priority is comfort and that doesn't only involve beds. It's about towels, carpet, armchairs and the humankind. A smile, a small joke, a helpful gesture from staff and genuine concern for your wellbeing. That is what will make me comfortable. I don't need anything fancy. (Although fancy is nice!)

I am a design fan no matter the budget. I want my Irish hotels to be distinctly Irish but not overly so. I don't care whether the hotel is functional and modern or elegant and old school. The design just needs to be thoughtful.

If the hotel is dated, so be it, but what has the team done to work around that? Do they make up for it in hospitality?

Finally, I need to see a team. A happy team of people who enjoy being in the hotel as much as their guests.

Hotels in Ireland are expensive compared to the US, even with a strong rate of exchange at the moment. In Dublin on certain dates, it compares to midtown Manhattan.

$$$$$ = Silly Money
$$$$ = Luxury but fair
$$$ = Somewhat budget conscious

Here are a few of my favorites (in no particular order).

Adare Manor, Adare, Co Limerick
Cost: $$$$$
www.adaremanor.com

This poster child five-star resort gets all the headlines in travel and golf press and for good reason. Gazillionaire JP McManus ploughed a lot of money into it and it shows. Everything from a round of golf to dining at Michelin-starred Oak Room or cocktails in the Tack Room is an experience, thoughtfully designed. I love the less posh (still expensive) Carriage House for food.

In many fancy resorts you get a fancy attitude, but not here. If you have the money to spend, check it out.

The Shelbourne, Dublin
Cost: $$$$$
www.theshelbourne.com

The Shelbourne is almost 200 years. I mean almost. In 2024, this iconic site will have crossed the 2-century mark. Dublin's great lady may seem dated but with its upscale refurb it has all modern conveniences. It is the perfect combination of posh and down to earth at the same time. Sitting on the doorstep of Saint Stephen's Green, it is essential Dublin whether you are overnighting or not. A pint in The Horseshoe or the 1824 is just Dublin 101. Watch for local, national and world class celebs or just watch Dubliners pop in for a coffee. Either way it is a slice of this unique city's life.

Marlfield House, Wexford
Cost: $$$$
www.marlfieldhouse.com

The Bowe ladies, Laura and Margaret have created the quintessential country house stay with a Regency-style manor in North Wexford. I love the library bar and cute dining room. I am also a mad fan of the Duck restaurant and new super design self-contained Pond Suites were covered by every style magazine in the country. Always classic but always ahead of its time, I love this spot.

Ariel House, Dublin
Cost: $$$
www.arielhouse.ie

With about 40 rooms, across three adjoining red-brick Victorian houses, Ariel House is more like a small hotel than a large family-owned B&B. It's right beside in the Aviva stadium, and under a mile from the city centre – in the posh area of Ballsbridge. With great breakfasts (and complimentary afternoon cakes and scones) and the warmest of welcomes, this is a great place to stay.

Hayfield Manor, Cork
Cost: $$$$$
www.hayfieldmanor.ie

I'm always amazed at how high-end hotels succeed in making me feel like I belong. I'm never comfortable in them and feel out of place with the "moneyed folk". Hayfield Manor has a country manor feel to it rather than splashy palace. It is a period house with subtle high-tech touches that you won't notice. The walled Garden and the excellent pool will wipe away any stresses. Orchids offers a beautiful fine dining menue but Perrott's is my haunt. It is family owned and classy to a fault.

Brooks Hotel, Dublin
Cost $$$$
www.brookshotel.ie

This Drury Street spot is my hidden gem. Whether you're in town for a weekend of shopping or a few days of clubbing, you will be able to stagger home and collapse on the most comfortable of beds oblivious that you are in the heart of the city. There's a rather random but fun, private cinema in the basement. The service and low key but attentive staff is the genius here. I don't like to share this place with many, but for you…

The Merchant, Belfast
Cost $$$$$
www.themerchanthotel.com

This Belfast five-star is a perfect match for the city of Belfast. I remember thinking it belonged there. Set in the former headquarters of the Ulster Bank, its 'Great Room' and Bert's Jazz Bar are just fun. Rooms are Victorian-style up front and Art Deco in the extension. The basement spa is an atmospheric space of candlelight and shadows. Think grand luxe everything, including the food (which, by the way, is fantastic) and the staff seemed just as ornate as the hardware.

The River Lee, Cork
Cost $$$$
www.doylecollection.com

The River Lee is part of the Doyle group with the bar set very high and it does not disappoint. On the face of it, it's a big, functional four-star, with an incredibly friendly and thorough service. It serves a fantastic breakfast in one of the most gorgeous salons, you will ever find. The bistro is excellent with a spectacular cocktail bar. I'm obsessed with the ode to Godot artwork in the lobby. Right on the river and a short stroll from the shops and pubs, I love this place. I will say it again. I love this place.

Kelly's Resort Hotel & Spa, Rosslare, Co Wexford
Cost: $$$$
www.kellys.ie

Full disclosure: This is a biased review. I've gone to Kelly's for years to experience something very special–a family-run business that equals anything more sophisticated elsewhere. With its confident but laid-back style, the same people come back year after year to experience a level of service that is rarely matched.

The easy décor with high end art (including a Warhol) walks that fine line between comfortable and stuffy. The light from the beach in the summer evenings that drifts to subtle and thoughtful evenings with excellent local seafood dinners and an incredible wine list makes this an out of the way and out of the park experience. It is almost guaranteed that you will be the only American staying here as it is a favorite of the well-to-do Irish.

The Ice House, Ballina, Co. Mayo
Cost: $$$
www.icehousehotel.ie

The Ice House is Victorian building near Ballina, once used as a store for wild salmon, with modern timber and glass extensions. This is a restful waterside retreat owned and run by a husband-and-wife team. The 32 light and spacious bedrooms have goose-down duvets and posh organic seaweed toiletries. Most have long views over the Moy river estuary to the wildlife and woodlands beyond. There is complimentary access to the hotel spa, with its outdoor cedar barrel sauna and two riverside hot tubs.

Gregans Castle, Ballyvaughan, Co Clare
Cost: $$$$
www.gregans.ie

First it isn't quite a castle but this haven in the heart of the Burren does something magical. My first experience was 24 years ago and the dinner I had that first night was one of the finest I have ever had. I even remember the Sequoia Grove cab I had. It is somehow other worldly once you enter the grounds but remains a truly Irish country house with sophisticated food and a fantastic wine list.

Great Southern Hotel, Killarney, Co Kerry
Cost: $$$
www.greatsouthernkillarney.com

Built in 1854 the Great Southern Hotel is a pillar of Killarney and indeed Irish hospitality. The Scally family who run Hayfield Manor have given this place the "je ne sais quoi" it needed. Grace Kelly and Jackie Kennedy have stayed here, and there is a nod to that era in the décor. If ever there was a grand lobby, it is here. I love the lounge and the "wine experience". The summer breakfast can be jammed with tour groups so wait until the fall. There is a great pool and gym. If you plan on business while in town this is probably not the place for you as the Wi-Fi isn't exactly speedy. However, there is something uniquely romantic about this place, so I am willing to forgive.

Brook Lodge & Macreddin Village, Aughrim, Co Wicklow
Cost: $$$$
www.brooklodge.com

There is a little magic to this mini village in Wicklow with babbling streams, ancient stone bridges, and lush rolling hills. It might be a little overdone and far too many weddings happen there, but I really like village inn feel. The hotel itself feels like someone's home. The organic restaurant with an emphasis on local produce is excellent as is the Wells spa.

Dingle Benners, Dingle, Co. Kerry
Cost: $$$
www.dinglebenners.com

The first thing you will see when you walk into Dingle Benners is Mrs. Benners Bar, whose book-lined walls, wooden floors, and antique Irish furniture create that warm welcome you need. It is a haven in a town that gets quite mad in the summer.

The hotel is bigger than you initially think. It has bright and cheery traditional décor that isn't groundbreaking but makes you feel good inside. Service is warm and friendly with a fantastic breakfast. Rooms are cozy and comfortable. Is this hotel exciting? No, but it is the perfect place to lay your head after a long day of sightseeing and several pints of merrymaking in Dingle town.

Killarney Park Hotel, Killarney, Co Kerry
Cost: $$$$$
www.killarneyparkhotel.ie

The very first stop on one of my Ireland with Michael tours, Killarney Park is like closing the door in the center of town to lock you away from the tourism noise. The key to this hotel is the staff. Whatever they do to make it happen, I have never seen such attentiveness without being annoying. It's all about tone here and whatever that is, they get it perfectly. Good luck getting a room there in the summer.

The Old Ground Hotel, Ennis, Co Clare
Cost: $$$

www.oldgroundhotelennis.com

I'm just back from a short stay The Old Ground Hotel and in truth I wasn't expecting very much. The Old Ground has been around a long time and with a central location it has always been hugely popular. My gut is that the welcome and the warmth of the staff is key here. I had a stellar dinner on my first evening. Old fashioned Irish food served with confidence and panache. The rooms aren't modern and perhaps a little dull, but the beds are comfortable, the pints gorgeous and smiles at reception, consistent. I love this place.

The Europe, Killarney, Co Kerry
Cost $$$$

www.theeurope.com

The Europe has the best spa and gym in the country, hands down. It has been carved into the ground with a glass roof and an outdoor pool with the best ever-changing view due to the light and half-light on Lough Lein. Their large and beautifully appointed rooms are a definite favorite of mine. Add to that, an extensive menu including beef and lamb from its own farm, and you have a world class establishment. Do not miss this place.

Ferrycarrig Hotel, Ferrycarrig, Co Wexford
Cost: $$$

www.ferrycarrighotel.ie

I've grown up in this hotel and if the walls could talk, I would be in trouble but year after year it has evolved into a thoughtfully designed establishment with excellent customer service. The view from the Slaney estuary gives an air of calm that revives the soul. Breakfast is top notch and watching the cormorant dining while hopping off your own "Full Irish" is unique to the hotel. The Ferrycarrig has an excellent gym and pool with a focus on families. I love their commitment to locally sourced, Wexford ingredients in their menus. The Dry Dock bar is a fun spot with live music.

My Pubs

How do I choose a pub? I could give you "high fallutin" nonsense about an incredible gastro experience involving pork smoked in the backyard during a full moon or a raspberry and nettle IPA brewed in the basement, but this is nonsense. I judge my pubs on 3 things:

The Pint
Does this pub understand the pint of Guinness. Does it throw it out at you without giving it the time it needs to settle? Do they look less than pleased if they serve something less than perfect? Do they give black gold, the respect it deserves? I don't want to order a Sex on the Beach in Ireland. Make sure the stout is perfect.

The Place
I hate an over designed pub. I want it to be shabby but not fake shabby and for sure not shabby chic. I still want the comfort. I want it to be easy. I don't want to be judged for being too old or too young. I don't want loud and I don't want a library.

The Grub
A good pub must have some food to serve with your pint, but I don't want to take it too seriously. I also don't want to be trendy. If I see the words locally sourced, sustainable, organic I am encouraged but if I read it every second line of the menu, it starts to get annoying. I also like the soup to be basic and chips are a must.

Here is a list of pubs I love. This could take a while. Let's start in Wexford. I have four.

Wexford

The Sky and the Ground
@theskyandtheground

Winner of this 2022 Irish Pub of the Year, this place named after a song by local legend Pierce Turner, gets it right. The perfect level of comfort, ease and shabby. Johnny and Nuala understand the assignment. It is welcoming but not overly so. The pint is gorgeous. Loads of nooks and crannies for some peace or to avoid having to be social. Dark but you don't need a white stick to get around.

The Sky and the Ground

Simon Lamberts
www.simonlambertandsons.ie

I've spent most of my adult life in this family-owned establishment, listening to opera singers and locals dissect the latest production at the nearby National Opera House. I've watched singers from all over the world flirt and sing. Simon's caters to a younger crowd now with their own brewery serving incredible beers. However, I still feel at home here. The food is incredible, high end without a high price and there's an ease to the place that makes you feel comfortable.
www.simonlambertandsons.ie

The Cape
mackensbar63@gmail.com

This stalwart in the Bull Ring is a gem in the heart of the town. Pub, grocer & undertaker, the place is unique to say the least. They serve a gorgeous pint, and you can sit at the window to watch Wexford pass by before you. Again, the place is shabby so there is an ease that cannot be faked.

The Cape Bar

Bugler Doyles
www.buglerdoyles.ie

Bugler Doyles is as unpretentious as it gets. There is nothing like sitting at the gorgeous front bar with a pint of Black listening to locals opine with the strongest of Wexford accents and flowery lingo. No food but with the Premier chipper across the road, who needs it. There is music on the weekends, and it just feels comfortable. They've also got small, very comfortable and budget conscious guest accommodations upstairs.

Dublin

Dublin pubs are different to establishments down the country. Dubliners are the best storytellers you will ever hear so finding that spot in the quiet of the afternoon to sit and listen to life happening is a required activity in the city.

Neary's
www.nearys.ie

The back door of Neary's leads to the stage door of the Gaiety theater, the iconic stage set into the corner of Stephen's Green. You don't need a reason to pop in here in the middle of your shopping adventure on Grafton Street. A quiet haven doesn't need to advertise. The stillness combined with the tiny snug and a pint of Arthur will give you the quintessential perfect sojourn in the heart of the city.

Neary's Pub

The Gravediggers

I've heard more than once that this place serves the best pint of stout in Dublin. My gut is that the place looks exactly like it did when it first opened. The furniture is as worn as the customers. I fit in perfectly. Pop in after a guided tour of Glasnevin Cemetery.

The Long Hall

@longhallpub

A perfect place to pop in for a pint while out and about in Dublin. When you step into the Long Hall Pub you will notice the beautiful Victorian charm in the décor including the handcrafted dark polished wood carvings all around, traditional snugs & golden details.

Donegal

The Smugglers Creek Inn

www.smugglerscreekinn.com

The Smugglers Creek Inn in Rossnowlagh is a pub that serves the most scenic pint you've ever seen, looking out across the magnificent Rossnowlagh beach and Donegal Bay.

Nancy's

@nancysbarardara

I also wholeheartedly endorse Nancy's in Ardara (pronounced ardraaaaah). Nancy's is a wandering kind of place with excellent unpretentious food and there always seems to be a story from locals and internationals alike. You will leave having talked to a stranger.

Athlone

Sean's Bar
www.seansbar.ie

Sean's Bar dates back to 900AD, a fact that was verified during an excavation in 1970. I was skeptical at first but in there you will see one of the original walls that was discovered during the excavation and remains on show in the pub. Coins that were also discovered, sit inside Dublin's National History Museum. They also distill their own whiskey

Sean's Bar

Derry

Peadar O Donnell's
@peadarsderry

I already recommended Peadar O Donnell's and indeed stopped by during our filming of the walled city. Make time for a pint in here. The pint is gorgeous and even better, there's also traditional and contemporary music played every night of the week, for those of you looking to go hopping about the place.

Down

Grace Neill's
www.graceoneills.com

Grace Neill's in Donaghadee in County Down is one of the oldest pubs in Ireland, with about 400 years to its name. First established in 1611 as 'The Kings Arms'. It was later named after Grace Neill, who was given the pub as a wedding present from her father. The establishment has been visited by 'smugglers, pirates, sailors and soldiers over the years' and there is also evidence of a ghost or two

Limerick

Dolans
www.dolans.ie

Dolans has hosted me on many's the night for late night sessions. The place is lived in. With trad music every night and decent, casual food, the place is always hoppin'.

Bobby Byrne's
www.bobbybyrnes.ie

Bobby Byrne's is one of those pubs that feels like home. It's warm and cozy with a lit fire. The pub was established by former Limerick mayor Bobby Byrne. Solid pub grub.

Nancy Blakes
@nancyblakesbar

Nancy Blakes is an old-world pub that is also modern. You will hear plenty of traditional music in here, but you will also witness throngs of youngsters in the beer garden out back.

The Roadside Tavern
www.roadsidetavern.ie

The Roadside Tavern, located on the main street of the small village of Lisdoonvarna, is one of the best traditional Irish pubs in Ireland. Along with the Tavern, the Burren Smokehouse is right there offering fine Irish smoked salmon. You can walk between the two in less than one minute.

Durty Nelly's
www.durtynellies.com

If you are looking for an authentic, traditional Irish pub, look no further than Durty Nelly's in Bunratty. Established in 1620, Nelly's has been serving pints for a while now. Is it touristy outside? Hell, yes but the wandering rooms inside are just gorgeous. Think low ceilings with massive timber beams covered in years of peat smoke hanging in the air

Durty Nelly's

Offaly

JJ Houghs Singing Pub
@jjhoughs

Trees and vines grow in and out of the windows of this legend among Irish pubs. For years, the place has been famed for its authentic Irish pub experience, a place of good times, superb music, and great beer too! The place is proudly odd and old fashioned, but you can get anything from stout to a decent cocktail. I guarantee you will have a story to tell when you leave.

Kerry

De Barra's Folk Club
www.debarra.ie

Known as the Carnegie Hall of Kerry, De Barra's Folk Club in Clonakilty is iconic, a musical history museum. The venue has played host to every Irish folk musician you can think. Enjoy the pint and take in the pub with walls covered with musical instruments from all over the world

Dick Macks
www.dickmackspub.com

Dick Macks is unique to say the least. Established in 1899, this iconic pub encompasses three key things: beer, whiskey and, unexpectedly, leather. This is another dual-function pub with its fine selection of drinks laid out on one half of the bar and a leather shop on the other. They've also got brewery tours.

South Pole Inn
www.southpoleinn.com

With a glacier and a mountain named for him, Tom Crean has quite the legacy including the South Pole Inn, which he opened in the early 1920s. Located in the sweet village of Annascaul, this pub is a perfect pitstop while on a jaunt around Dingle. The inside is covered with maps, photos and all kinds of polar memorabilia in celebration of the three-time Antarctic explorer. A fascinating stop.

Galway

Galway is mad for pubs. You are tripping over them. I recommend just a few.

Tigh Neachtains
www.tichneachtain.com

Tigh Neachtains is a favorite of locals for both food and this place on the corner of Cross Street has been open since 1894. There will be mad crowds at their live music sessions or head there earlier to get a place outside in their sunny drinks area to people watch.

The Crane
www.thecranebar.com

The Crane is another spot for trad music. Upstairs is the spot for it. Get there early as even standing room is limited.

Concert Halls and Theatres

When in Ireland, be sure to check out our vibrant theatre and concert scene. It is the perfect snapshot of modern Irish life with everything from classic Irish drama, musical theatre, opera to rock, folk and traditional music.

The National Concert Hall (Dublin)
www.nch.ie

The National Concert Hall, just off St. Stephen's Green in the middle of Georgian Dublin, is one of Ireland's National Cultural Institutions and the venue for classical music in the country. The main auditorium, in what was once a university examination hall, holds about 1,200 people—though perhaps its most impressive feature is the massive organ behind the stage. This is a concert hall featuring concert and symphony orchestras, classical voices, and high-end performances. Smaller recitals for up to 250 people are hosted in the adjoining John Field Room, while the Carolan Room, named after the 17th-century blind Irish harpist that I blather on about a lot on the tv show, is occasionally used for performances and has a capacity of 100. If you are in Dublin for a few nights, this is where you will find Ireland's finest classical artists.

The National Opera House (Wexford)
www.nationaloperahouse.ie
www.wexfordopera.com

While we have the newly formed and incredibly dynamic Irish National Opera based in Dublin, I say, the best time to see opera is at the Wexford Festival Opera in Wexford town at the National Opera House. The space was built in 2008 on the site of the old Theatre Royal and frankly, you won't find a better hall in Ireland. (I sang on opening night!) It is a world-class venue presenting Irish and international events, opera, music, family events, comedy, theatre and dance all year outside of the world-renowned opera festival in late October. It holds 2 performance spaces, the O'Reilly Theatre and the Jerome Hynes Theatre.

Bord Gais Theatre (Dublin)
www.bordgaisenergytheatre.ie

Housed in an awkward angular, Daniel Libeskind–designed building in the trendy docklands area of the city, the Bord Gais Theatre has a 2,000-plus capacity, making it Ireland's biggest theater. Its calendar includes the best of international ballet, classical music, pop gigs, and musicals. If you want to see a West End touring show, this is the place. It also hosts the incredible Irish National Opera.

The Bord Gais Theatre

The Gaiety Theatre (Dublin)
www.gaietytheatre.ie

Since 1871, The Gaiety Theatre has been the heart of Dublin opera, musicals, drama, revues, comedy, concerts, dance, festivals, and pantomime. The Grand Old Lady of South King Street just off Stephen's Green has remained a vital and ever-changing expression of Irish culture. It is as Dublin as you get. Home to Riverdance every summer, I wholeheartedly recommend a trip. Being an old hall, comfort is not its strong suit and if you have long legs I would check with the ticket office about seats with some space in front of them. Still, all year you will find something interesting playing there and more than that, the place is iconic. If you are there mid-Summer, book early.

Riverdance at the Gaiety Theatre

The Abbey Theatre (Dublin)
www.abbeytheatre.ie

Although the Abbey Theatre looks quite contemporary, even postmodern with its glass front, the performance venue has turn-of-the-century origins. In truth I don't love the place as I think it doesn't justify the incredible work that happens on the stage. Famed poet, W.B. Yeats, along with another Irish writer, Lady Augusta Gregory, opened the national theater in 1904. It's since been rebuilt and now features 630 seats and a continuous roster of Ireland's best and brightest playwrights. If you want to see Friel, Carr, Synge, Behan then this is the place to find it.

The Gate (Dublin)
www.gatetheatre.ie

The Gate is a Georgian wonder designed by Richard Johnston in 1784 as an assembly room for the Rotunda Hospital next door. The Gate has been one of Dublin's most important theaters since its founding in 1929 by Micheál MacLiammóir and Hilton Edwards, who also founded Galway City's An Taibhdhearc as the national Irish-language theater. It stages many established productions by Irish as well as foreign playwrights—and plenty of huge actors have performed here, including Orson Welles (his first paid performance). There is always something interesting to see here.

Cork Opera House (Cork)
www.corkoperahouse.ie

Cork Opera House is the premier venue in Cork city for the best concerts, comedy, drama, dance, family fare, and, of course, opera. Located in the heart of Cork City, the Opera House has been a Cork cultural institution for over 160 years. They've an ongoing jazz series in their smaller green room. The place is packed all year with events, so you are spoiled for choice when in town.

INEC (County Kerry)
www.inec.ie

When in Kerry the place to check out is the INEC at Gleneagles Hotel in Killarney. All summer they have shows catering to tourists but all year you will find a full schedule of national and international artists of every genre.

Glor (County Clare)
www.glor.ie

Glor in Ennis is the heart of theatre in County Clare, a cultural complex that seems to be ever expanding. Irish artists dominate here with a real commitment to Clare talent with folk, classical, country playing all year. Check out the roster while you are in town.

Siamse Tire (County Kerry)
www.siamsatire.com

Siamse Tire, the National Folk Theater of Ireland has been around for 50 years and based in Tralee, also in County Kerry. From October to April, it hosts a wide range of events including touring drama, classical music, comedy, dance, and opera along with productions by local groups and musical societies. Folk Art has been handed down across generations over 50 years through their National Folk Theatre Training Academy.

The Druid Theatre Company (Galway)
www.druid.ie

The Druid Theatre Company, referred to as The Druid, is THE theatre company, based in Galway. As well as touring extensively across Ireland, the company's productions have played internationally including Lincoln Center and on Broadway. Druid is a pioneer in the development of Irish theatre and is credited with making Galway one of the primary cultural centers in Ireland. With legendary Tony® winner, Garry Hynes at the helm, you really shouldn't miss a stop when in Galway.

The Druid Theatre

Heading Home

Duty Free, Check in, and Covid Protocols

Dublin, along with most airports globally, has had its fair share of post covid hitches. In truth, pre-Covid the service in the airport has been up and down. While I actually love the Duty-Free options and the way the new terminal is designed, getting to that side of security, and checking in bags beforehand is quite traumatic. Latest recommendations are allowing 3 hours for check in before crossing the Atlantic. That is actually my norm, so it doesn't make any difference to me. I love airports and like to be early.

If you plan on submitting your receipts to get your tax back allow yourself up to 3.5 hours. Yes, it is a pain in the arse but think of the cold hard cash in your pocket rather than in the pocket of the Irish government. For VAT refunds head to the clearly marked counter area. Submit receipts that hopefully you have gathered and put in an envelope. Fill out the accompanying paperwork and that's it. You can also use the Horizon Card which simplifies it. Go to www.shoptaxfree.com.

Be sure to check in online before you get to the airport. Find your airline and be prepared to complete immigration pre-check in line to check in. At this point you will get to hand over the luggage and head upstairs by escalator to the line for security. If you buy a fast-track pass or are flying business you won't have too much hardship, but I have seen hundreds of people in line at this point waiting to squeeze through an overstressed, understaffed security stop.

One clear advantage when flying to the U.S. on Aer Lingus (or indeed any other airline) is that you clear customs and immigration in Dublin or Shannon and land at a domestic terminal in the U.S. This is especially useful if you're flying into a very busy airport where this process can take hours on a bad day if you don't have Global Entry. This way you literally land at your arrival gate, let's say, Chicago and change gates in that terminal. No long wait for customs or immigration after a long-haul flight.

Pre-clearance in Dublin while convenient, when you look back, is quite the trial before you take off. If you don't time it right, the queue can be very long. If you are a Business Class passenger you can fast track a security lane, but no matter how posh your seat is, there is no premium line for U.S. immigration. It can be a long haul, especially in those summer months when every Irish American that ever existed is in the same room as you. Still, you need to keep it in mind that you are getting it over with, rather than dealing with it after 8 hours on a cramped flight.

It would be unfair to say that it is the worst wait in the world given that most people would queue longer at U.S. immigration in JFK, O Hare, or Dallas. At the worst we are talking 45 minutes.

If you are a planner and like to be early, like me, you will forge on and think of the cuppa at the end of it at the gate or at "51st & Green" the pre-clearance lounge (Ireland being seen as the green 51st state of America).

The pre-clearance lounge is located at the far end of the departure lounge. It is quite the hike, and it will indeed feel like an oasis of sorts once you get there. There is free access if you are flying business, but the walk-up price is €39. I think that if the regular gates are packed and you are early this is not bad at all.

The lounge does get busy, but it is airy and bright. I prefer my lounges to have low lights and be a bit more muted but the circular lounge with glass everywhere has a light and breezy feel with plenty of cozy corners. They have a great little buffet and there is a barista on hand to serve frothy coffees or something stronger to get that final boozy moment before leaving Ireland.

Glossary of Gaelic Phrases

While you won't hear Gaelic used in everyday language outside of the Gaeltacht or Irish speaking areas in Donegal, Kerry, Galway, or Mayo, nearly everyone uses the occasional phrase in everyday conversation. Here are a few for you to try when you are there.

English	_Gaelic_	_Pronunciation_
Please	Le do thoil	Leh du hull
Thank You	Go raibh maith agat	Guh rev mah a gut
What is your name?	Cad is ainm duit	Cod iss anum ditt
Where is the bathroom	Cá bhfuil an leithreas	Caw will on leh ress
My name is Michael	Michael is aimn dom	Michael iss anum dumb
How are you?	Conas atá tú	Cunass ataw two
I am well	Tá mé go maith	Taw may guh mah
What time is it?	Cén t'am é?	Cain towm eh?
Cheers	Sláinte	Slawin cheh
You're gorgeous	Tá tú go h'alainn	Taw two guh hawling
Hello	Dia dhuit	Deea gwit
Goodbye	Slán	Slawn

Acknowledgements

When I think about writing a thank you note for this book I have to laugh. I wasn't exactly top of the English class at the Christian Brothers School in Wexford. I still struggle with sentence structure, let alone writing a chapter with some form.

I had help. I didn't have a ghost writer, but I have an entire "Ireland with Michael" team who helped me with research, and who got information on hotels and tourism sites. I had help sourcing photos. I had help correcting my grammar and typesetting.

It is with much gratitude that I acknowledge these people here:

Ben and Rosemary for sourcing all of the hard-to-reach information. It was tedious and endless.

John Michael and Michael for your commitment from day one (and for the awful jokes).

Phyllis for correcting my grammar and making everything look pretty.

Majella for all your help with social media.

Jean for your tireless work, your strong work ethic and for making me laugh every time we talk.

Steve for believing in me.

Ben, again, for writing the tv show and for thinking like an Irish fella.

Mike for always smiling and for the endless hours in the attic.

Thank you to Aer Lingus, CIE Tours and Tourism Ireland for their sponsorship and support.

A huge thank you to you, for supporting us. We intend to be around for a long time, and we couldn't do it without you.

Finally, to Alfie, Billy, and Mark for every welcome home.

To learn more about vacations to Ireland with Michael, call 1.800.486.4816 or go to www.irelandwithmichael.com